£5.95

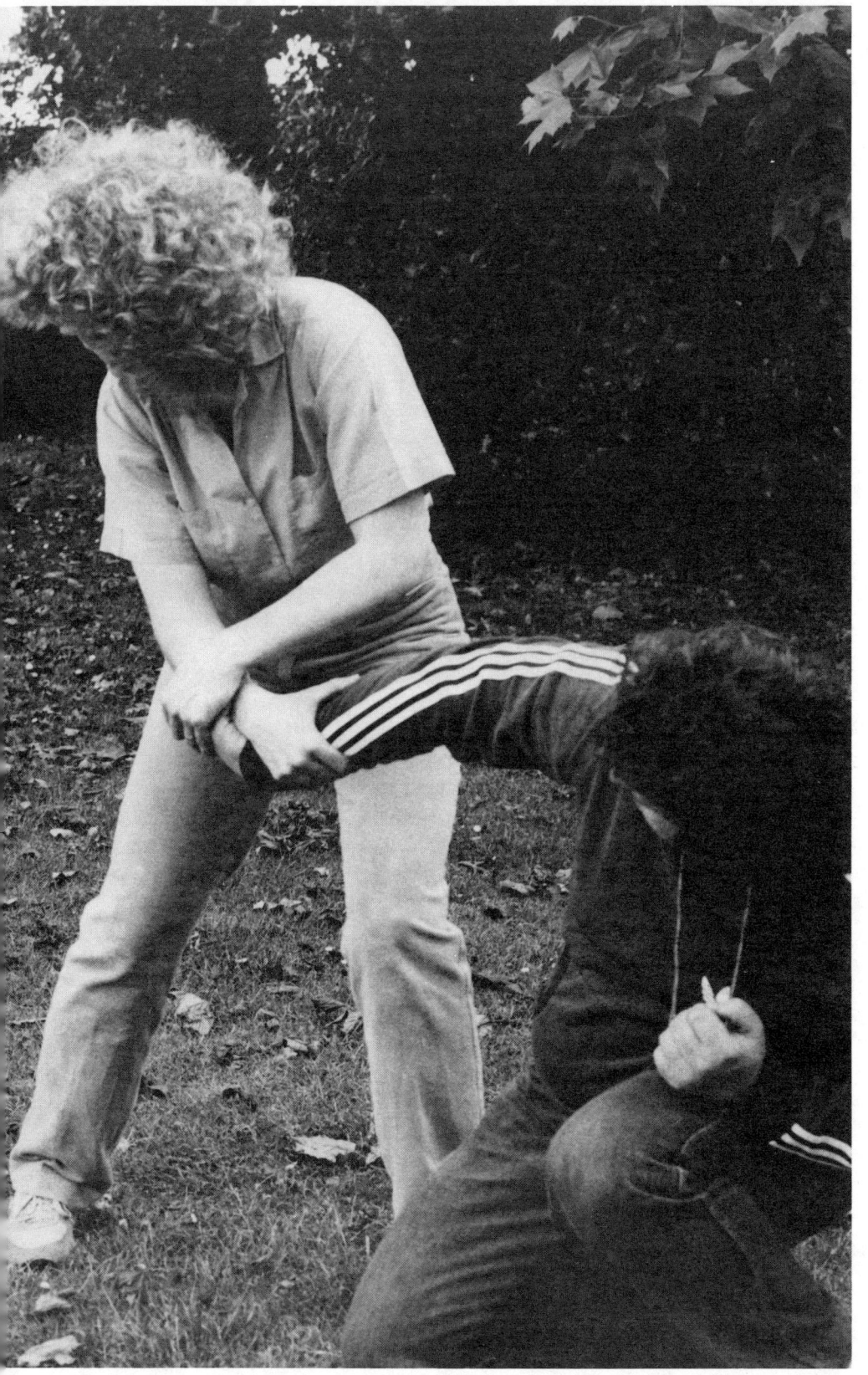

THE OFFICIAL SELF DEFENCE HANDBOOK

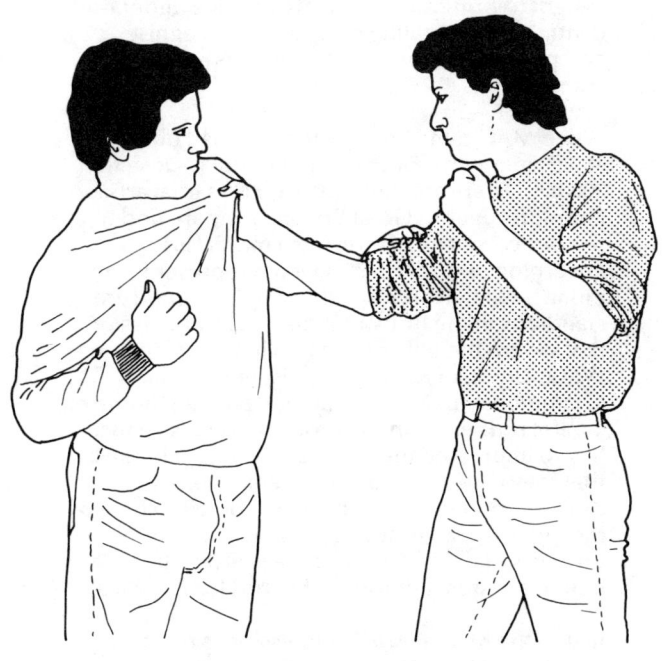

The Martial Arts Commission is the governing body for all the martial arts in Britain. It was set up in 1977 at the request of the Minister for Sport, the Sports Council, the Departments of Employment and the Environment, the Home Office and the martial arts themselves. All were concerned at the uncontrolled proliferation of unqualified 'teachers' with large followings, and sought to bring all martial arts practice under one central authenticating body which recognises competence and administers events and competitions.

When MAC came into existence, it had only 16,000 members, but now that figure is close to 100,000. There are more than 4,000 martial arts clubs throughout Great Britain. They are under the direct control of individual martial art governing bodies, each of which represents the pinnacle of that art's development. So good are standards in the British Martial Arts Commission that we are the only nation to win the prestigious World Union of Karate Organisations Team Championship twice – beating Japan (the home of karate) four times in the process! MAC's jiu jitsu has so impressed the oriental governing bodies that they have offered immediate recognition to British exponents. British aikido contains some of the highest grades outside of Japan and forms the basis of the highly effective police self defence system authorised by the Home Office.

Just as the Martial Arts Commission is the only source of martial art excellence in Britain, so it is also the only body capable of producing this definitive book on self defence.

THE Martial Arts Commission of Great Britain

THE OFFICIAL SELF DEFENCE HANDBOOK

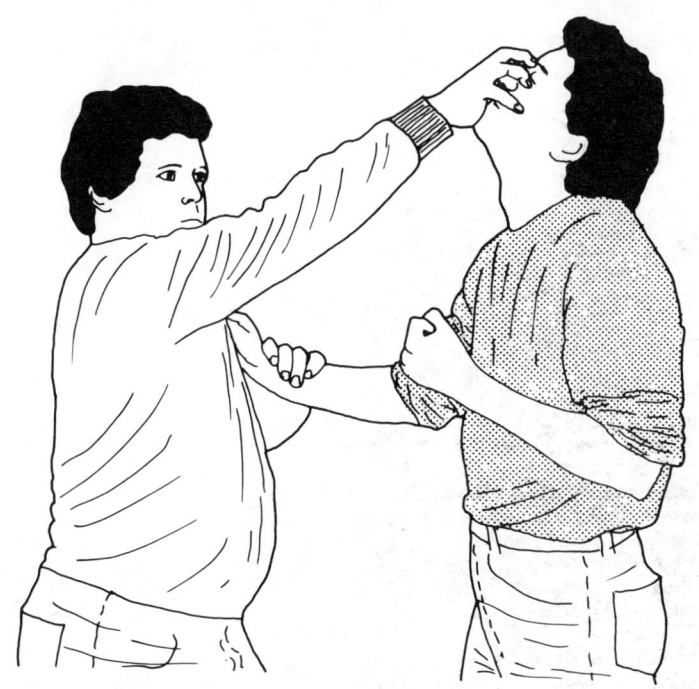

BY DAVID MITCHELL

Pelham

First published in Great Britain by Pelham Books Ltd,
44 Bedford Square, London WC1B 3DP 1985

© Antler Books Ltd 1985
11 Rathbone Place, London W1P 1DE

All Rights Reserved. No part of this publication
may be reproduced, stored in a retrieval system,
or transmitted, in any form or by any means,
electronic, mechanical, photocopying, recording
or otherwise, without the permission of the
copyright owner.

British Library Cataloguing in Publication Data

Mitchell, David, 1944 –
  MAC self defence handbook
  1. Martial arts
  I. Title   II. Martial Arts Commission
  796.8   GV1101

ISBN 0 7207 1586 5
ISBN 0 7207 1591 1 pbk

Designed by Ian Hughes
Line illustrations by MJL Cartographics
Photography by Mike O'Neill, Take 3
Picture on p. 8 © Peter Cook
Typesetting by Fakenham Photosetting Ltd.
Colour separation by Prestige Graphic Services Ltd.
Printed and bound by Hazell Watson & Viney Ltd.

CONTENTS

Foreword
by B Whelan, Chairman of the Martial Arts Commission   7

Introduction   9
Martial arts, combat sports, and self defence · Self defence courses — the pitfalls · Thumps versus twists · Self defence — the options available · The scope of self defence.

Section 1 Theory
The law and self defence	16
Weapons and self defence	21
Realism in self defence	25
Assertion	30
Awareness and avoidance	33

Theory · Playing it safe · In conclusion.

Section 2 Practical (1) Basic techniques
Timing	41
Blocks and evasions	45
Body weapons and targets	51
Development of force	60

Section 3 Practical (2) Simple responses to attacks
First echelon responses	70
Second echelon responses	81
Strikes · Grapples.	
Practical responses	96

Section 4 Practical (3) Putting techniques and responses into practice
Escapes	110
Low key responses	118
Basic ground work	119

Section 5 General advice for students
Practising self defence	128

Aikido · Full contact · Hapkido · Karate · Kempo · Kendo · Kung fu · Taekwondo · Tang soo do · Thai boxing.

Fit to practise	136
Safe to practise	142
The Martial Arts Commission	145
Useful contacts	147
About the book	148
The MAC self defence course complete syllabus	150
Simple analysis of attacks and responses	152

FOREWORD

Until now, anyone who wanted to learn effective self defence had to join a martial arts club. In 1984, the Martial Arts Commission decided to pool its considerable technical resources to see whether a worthwhile basic self defence course could be designed. This book is the product.

Previous self defence books were drawn from a single martial art discipline; this one embraces them all. The high energy striking techniques of karate are incorporated with the evasion and joint locks of aikido, and the short range jolting strikes of kung fu combine with the throws of jiu jitsu. They produce a unique system representing the most effective basic self defence that can be taught in a short period.

The most significant difference between this book and others is that it is based upon a system. The MAC self defence course is not a mere compendium of techniques. Those selected for inclusion follow each other in a logical sequence that can be quickly learnt.

Brian Eustace is a 6th dan black belt in aikido (a 6th dan is a mark of very great competence). He is also a retired police officer and a Home Office approved instructor, responsible for the training of Britain's police self defence coaches. He has designed and operates a police self defence system to meet the stringent standards laid down by the Home Office Police Training Unit.

Unlike most martial arts instructors concerned with self defence, Brian Eustace has faced violence many times as part of his normal duties and is better qualified than most to know both what is involved and what really works. He has very kindly adapted his system to make it suitable for our MAC self defence course. Therefore I commend this book to you as the Martial Arts Commission's official basic self defence handbook.

B Whelan
Chairman, Martial Arts Commission

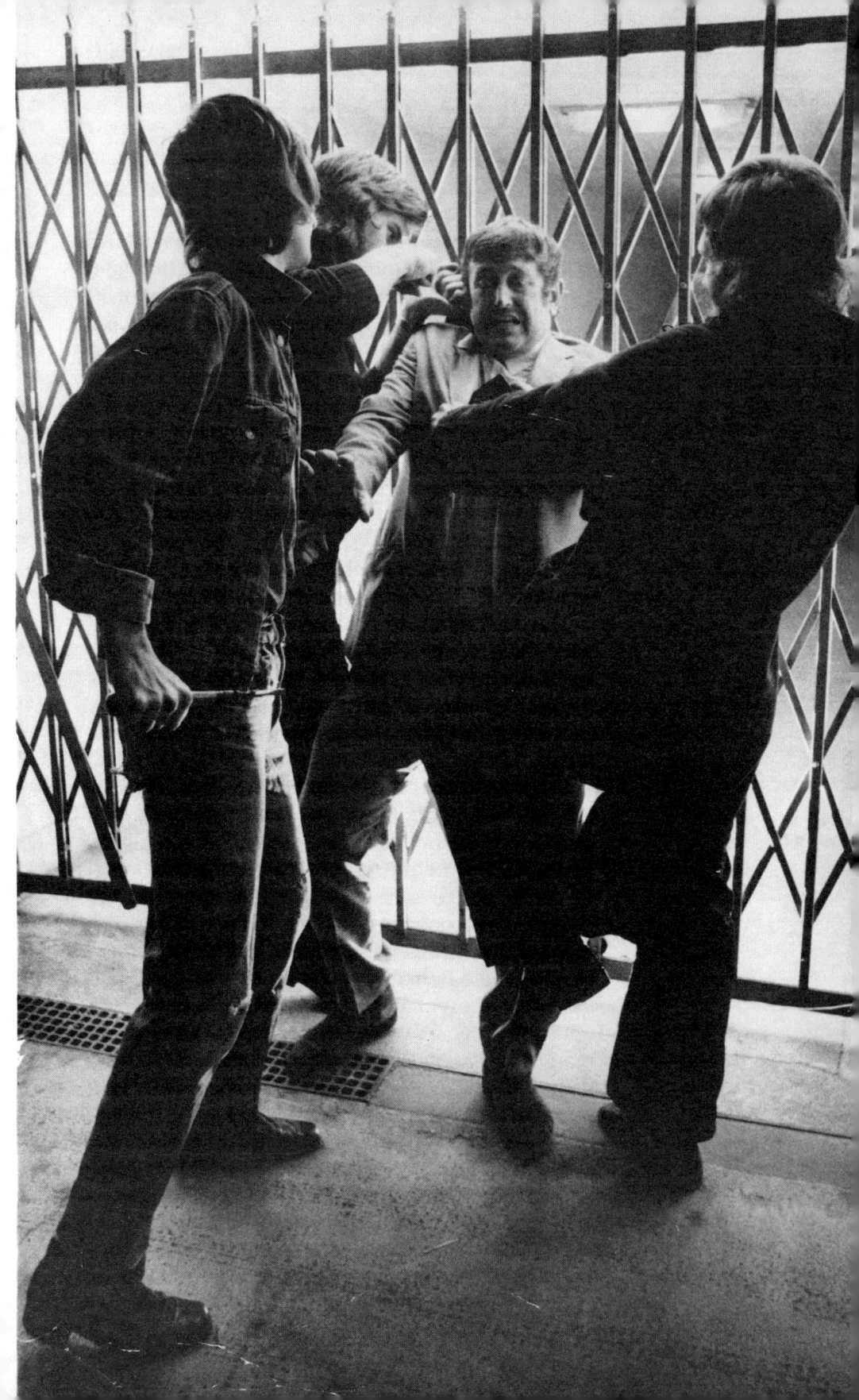

INTRODUCTION

Martial arts, combat sports and self defence

In times of war, the battlefield presents an opportunity to test military techniques or martial arts. Those widely known in Britain come from the Orient where there is a love of tradition. Some martial arts are practised today much as they were a thousand years ago. Others have altered to meet changing requirements. Some have shed the more dangerous techniques and become combat sports, where regular sparring between partners develops fighting techniques so they become more effective in that sporting context.

Unarmed combat is one part of the martial arts. It exists in many forms, both ancient and modern, and its aim is to capture, incapacitate, or kill an opponent. One of its uses is to allow a soldier to continue fighting effectively when he has lost his gun.

Self defence is the name given to any of a great number of systems based on an adapted martial art or combat sport. Since both are systems of fighting, it follows that their techniques can be applied in a non-military, non-sporting context such as self defence. The success of this application can only be guessed at since few people regularly face situations where such a response is necessary. Consequently, unlike the case of martial art or combat sport, there is no opportunity to test its effectiveness in the field.

To test self defence systems, it is necessary to analyse the outcome of many attacks. By this means, it would be theoretically possible to select the combat sport or martial art techniques which actually work. If these were put together in a teaching system, the world's first true short self defence course would come about.

One group of people with more experience in self defence than any other is the police. However, the techniques policemen use are restricted to what is

INTRODUCTION

acceptable; this means no punching or kicking. Members of the public are not so restricted, and the scope of techniques can therefore be widened. By drawing from the knowledge of a police self defence instructors' coach and by including additional effective techniques supplied by experts in the martial arts and combat sports, it has been possible to go some way towards developing a short self defence system.

Learning self defence – some useful guidelines

The goal of training in a martial art, combat sport, or pure self defence system is to reach a stage where the body can react instinctively to an attack, for it is no use trying to remember which hand grasps what when fists are flying. With hard and prolonged training, conditioned reflexes are formed. These high speed automatic reactions necessary for self preservation require no conscious decision. Training must therefore be long enough for students to learn the techniques thoroughly. Obviously the more complicated the techniques, the longer the training must be.

The ideal self defence system would consist of one technique which worked every time, no matter what, but there is no such thing. The best self defence courses we can achieve will set out to use as few techniques as possible, with new ones grudgingly added only after they passed the tests of simplicity, effectiveness, and wide application.

With any technique, there is likely to be a highly effective manner of performance – which may take ten years to acquire. A slightly less effective version can perhaps be learnt in twelve weeks. The first option will be selected for the martial art or combat sport, but the second is more logical for the shorter self defence course.

Some self defence techniques are simple to use and highly effective but cannot be generally taught. One such example is spear hand to the eyes. In this technique, the fingers are stiffened and their tips driven with a fair degree of force into the attacker's eyeballs. It is possible to become good at it in a short time by practising on pigs' heads bought from the butchers. However, this suggestion revolts normal people, so the technique cannot be considered for the general self defence course.

Self defence courses – the pitfalls
The average self defence course is no more than a grab-bag of clever techniques. Better courses are arranged systematically, in a sensible order – what to do when the attacker is standing away, what to do when he is close enough to grapple with, and what to do when taken to the floor.

Many frequently taught techniques are very specific. If a successful technique depends on being in the correct stance, with the correct foot forward, and with the attacker doing exactly what is expected, then it is as well to forget it. It is better to use a spontaneous, natural response than to fumble with a half learned technique.

If the attack is wrongly shown, the response suggested will also be incorrect. For example, many self defence systems show an attacker holding a knife in the front hand, but in practice this is unlikely to happen. Other systems have the attacker obligingly remaining still while the response is applied. Some self defence instructors have a favourite technique and go so far as to design an attack to show its use to the best effect.

It is important to avoid overconfidence. A technique practised competently enough with a willing partner in a warm and comfortable gymnasium may not work out in a cold dark street. A clever follow-through may be foiled when a real attacker does not produce the expected response. Some women's self defence schools are single sex and students never get to practise with a large, aggressive man. Other schools kit their students out in special tunics which allow a greater range of movement than everyday clothes. A good self defence course will avoid these pitfalls.

Thumps versus twists
It is easier to learn to kick someone in the groin than to capture and hold a flailing arm, but despite the shorter time needed to learn a pure striking system, it

remains very restricted in its application and suffers from numerous drawbacks. Enough energy must be put into a strike to make it effective. Often this means a run-up that can be seen and avoided. The run-up also needs distance in which the striking limb can accelerate; this may not be possible in a confined space.

The strike has to land on a vulnerable target and do so without causing injury to the user. Although a punch is a notoriously bad striking weapon, it remains the most common. Most people find it very difficult to form an effective fist, as the lower finger joints protrude beyond the knuckles and the wrist bends on impact. In the first case, the fingers are injured; in the second, the wrist can break.

Grappling techniques require not only more skill than strikes, but also physical strength. When a small person puts a joint lock on a stronger opponent, the leverage applied has to cause sufficient pain to stop further attack. This can be done in two ways. Either great physical strength can be applied to a large joint, or less strength (but strength nevertheless) to a smaller joint. By adjusting the leverage, the person attacked can control the assailant more effectively by varying the degree of pain inflicted. With a striking technique, that degree of control is absent.

Self defence – the options available

No single martial art or combat sport can claim a monopoly of effective self defence techniques. Each specialises in part of the self defence arsenal, developing that part to a very high degree. Japanese karate, for example, concentrates on striking techniques to the exclusion of grapples. Aikido, on the other hand, ignores the value of strikes and teaches highly effective joint locks and throws.

Some martial arts incorporate material which is superfluous for people who want a short self defence course and will not wish to learn how to disarm swordsmen or how to meditate. Other martial arts are so rich in practical material that they require ten or more years' study to master. Nevertheless, practice of any martial art or combat sport over the

INTRODUCTION

course of several years will lead to a good knowledge of self defence.

A properly constructed self defence course will deal only with the practical and relevant. Even so, there must be enough time to allow an adequate level of competence to be reached. This can vary from individual to individual and from course to course, but no less than 30 hours is necessary for the most elementary level.

The scope of self defence
Self defence, like unarmed combat, is at its best when taught to physically fit and aggressive young people. Physical fitness involves co-ordination, mobility and a degree of physical strength, all of which are vital to successful and wide ranging self defence. Without reasonable fitness, this can be effective in only a small number of cases.

Although self defence courses are available for children, they have little value. No child can ever hope to fend off an aggressive adult and there is a real danger that he will apply on classmates the techniques he has learnt. Only courses which teach escape from holds and evasion should be considered. In the long run, however, it is far better to enrol children in a good combat sport or martial art club. The techniques learned there are carefully structured to the child's ability and nature. Their practice will encourage the nervous child to resist bullying without placing other children at risk.

Old people with diminished physical fitness cannot expect to learn a self defence system with wide application and it is wrong to suggest they can. The same comments apply to those suffering physical disabilities. A person in a wheelchair has neither the mobility nor the stability to deal with many attacks. He cannot deliver effective kicks, nor use the hips to generate force in a strike or leverage in a throw. A sitting position takes away direct access to the attacker's vulnerable points, and the wheelchair reduces opportunities for both evasion and body positioning. The disabled or old person who feels in need of self defence is advised to take a course specialising in the use of weapons of convenience, such as walking sticks. Provided there is adequate justification for their use, they provide physically disadvantaged people with the best means of self defence available.

Slightly-built people are also generally at a disadvantage. In the case of striking techniques, a heavy person can generate sufficient force to stop the attacker relatively easily with even a slow-moving blow, but a smaller person must accelerate the strike to a much higher velocity to achieve the same impact. Grappling techniques require strength, even when they are applied with large leverage angles to small joints. There are many cases on record where a strong attacker has countered the leverage applied by a weaker person simply by unwinding his arm from what should have been a painful restraint hold.

In putting together the MAC course, care has been taken to choose techniques which work for most able-bodied people – provided enough time is spent on learning and practising them. Additional techniques are included for stronger people; these cases are identified by a comment.

The victim's attitude is always a significant factor in self defence. The coward armed with the finest self defence techniques in the world remains a coward. The aggressive victim, on the other hand, will be able to use that emotion to power physical self defence techniques to defeat even a persistent attacker. There are reported cases where physically disabled or old people have driven off attacks against all odds, through sheer indomitable spirit. Lack of physical size or fitness can be more than compensated for by a strong spirit.

Half-hearted responses can be dangerous. There is some evidence to show that feeble or ineffectual attempts at self defence may result in an escalation of force from the attacker. The victim must decide whether to co-operate with the attacker or to resist, though there is, of course, no guarantee that the person who submits will live through the experience. If resistance is chosen, then the physical response must be total, with no hold-back. Techniques must be used with nothing less than maximum force and maintained without stopping until

INTRODUCTION

the attacker retreats, clearly defeated.

Knowledge of the best self defence techniques in the world cannot guarantee that students will be able to defend themselves. They may be physically competent but, when faced with real aggression and the possibility of injury, become unable to cope and therefore suffer as badly as the untrained victim. There is a chance, however, that an effective response may be made. For this alone, a good self defence course could prove worth while.

SECTION 1 THEORY

THE LAW AND SELF DEFENCE

According to the law, assault need not entail actual violence; it is enough to threaten it and cause the victim apprehension. The victim cannot, however, resort to physical methods of self defence unless battery is involved. 'Battery' is the term used to describe physical force accompanying assault.

The law says that a person who is being attacked has the right to defend himself, using as much force as is reasonable to nullify the attack. 'Nullify' means that the attacker is brought up short and prevented from causing injury to the victim. In a typical case, the attacker has swung a punch and the victim avoids and catches the arm, twisting it into a restraint hold that prevents further attack.

Care must be taken to avoid using too much force when applying the hold, otherwise the victim might be the one arrested for assault and battery. Reasonableness is a subjective matter, and what seems reasonable in an adrenalin-provoking fight may not seem so two months later in a courtroom. The court always has the advantage of 20/20 hindsight.

What is reasonable can be illustrated by two hypothetical cases. In the first, a strong man is attacked by a young boy. It is in order for the man to protect himself from injury, provided that in doing so he causes no injury to the boy. He may, for instance, hold both the boy's arms firmly so the attack is nullified. If the boy becomes injured through his own actions during this restraint, the man cannot be held responsible because his response to the attack was reasonable. He may not, however, blind the boy or strike him with a weapon of convenience, such as a carving knife or milk bottle.

THE LAW AND SELF DEFENCE

Your response must be sufficient to nullify and not necessarily to wound an attacker

In the second case, a frail old man is attacked by a gang of hooligans brandishing weapons and obviously bent on doing him serious injury. Under these circumstances, he could be excused for taking up a weapon of convenience, such as his walking stick, and laying out those who come within reach. He would not be expected to adhere to the Queensberry rules.

In both these examples, the amount of force used in meeting the attack is reasonable, having regard to the nature of the attack. Is it likely that the strong man could have received serious injury through the boy's ineffectual attack? The answer must be 'No', and therefore the reasonable force required to restrain him is small. Is it likely that the old man

THE LAW AND SELF DEFENCE

would have been savagely beaten by the armed hooligans? It is indeed a possibility, and the reasonable force needed to protect him is considerable.

Reasonableness must apply, whatever the circumstances. If a person is attacked in his own home, the level of response must be appropriate to the circumstances. If an intruder is discovered, he can be challenged if it is safe to do so. If he is armed, or there is more than one, it is better to try to escape from the house and call for help. The householder should not take up a weapon unless he intends to use it effectively. Weapons can be taken away from unsure hands and used by the intruder. The householder is not entitled to injure an intruder except in defence of life or limb.

If a physical self defence response is necessary, care should be taken to make sure no damage is caused to third parties or their property. It is better to throw the attacker to the floor than through a plate-glass shop window. If a fight breaks out in a confined space, such as a dance floor or a lift, it is a good idea to turn away, guarding the face with the hands and closing the knees tightly together. If the place is crowded, the unarmed attacker will not be able to strike very hard and the worst injury inflicted will be a bruise.

If two people are fighting, it is never a good idea to try to separate them physically unless help is available. If one person is being assaulted, assistance can be given to try to prevent further injury.

Martial artists and those who study combat sports are in an invidious position when they are involved in violence. The courts seem to recognise only one class of martial artist — the expert, to whom they attribute superhuman powers.

Martial artists therefore have to be extremely careful when responding to attack. Take the example of a young black belt going with his girlfriend to the local disco, where she was insulted by two young men. The black belt complained to the manager, whereupon the two troublemakers were thrown out. They waited for him to leave and then attacked him. The black belt kicked one in the head, breaking his jaw, and punched the other, breaking three ribs. He was

THE LAW AND SELF DEFENCE

subsequently found guilty of causing actual bodily harm, despite the fact his two attackers were members of an amateur boxing club.

People who practise martial arts and combat sports are recommended to go to great lengths to avoid trouble. When avoidance is impossible, they should make every effort to use techniques which are unlikely to cause serious injury.

Police officers are similarly constrained. Their self defence manual contains techniques approved by the Home Office. If a person is injured by the police during an arrest, the Home Office will supply expert testimony to say that the arresting technique was approved. If the officer uses a non-standard technique, this testimony is unavailable and the case must be argued on other grounds.

Impact techniques are not easily controlled and a high energy strike to a vulnerable target can cause severe injury or even death. A blow to the head can cause unconsciousness, and if the victim falls and bangs his head on a solid floor, serious injury can result. Throws can prove dangerous for the same reasons. Any technique, however reasonable as a self defence response, may have an unforeseen outcome out of all proportion to what would normally have been expected.

In selecting the techniques to be used in the MAC course, careful attention has been paid to the liabilities incurred by using them. The eye-strike that opens many of the self defence sequences uses a grazing action of relaxed fingers and not a spearing thrust which would cause terrible damage.

Grappling techniques are more acceptable under the law because they are more easily controlled. Unfortunately, they take a long time to learn, and can be used successfully only by a fairly strong person. An attacker who is drunk or using drugs may have his pain threshold artificially heightened, so a restraint hold applied even to the point of fracture may not stop him. The only recourse in such a case is to knock him unconscious.

If the attacker produces a weapon and appears ready to use it, the victim is entitled to take stronger defensive action than if his assailant was unarmed.

This does not mean *carte blanche*; the response will depend on the weapon produced. If the attacker takes up a broom handle, the defender may not stab him mortally with a sword. If, on the other hand, a dagger or carving knife is produced, the defender may well be entitled, after a warning has been given and disregarded, to stab the attacker in the leg or arm.

There are two classes of weapons: those which are offensive in themselves and those which are not designed as weapons but can be so used. Class 1 offensive weapons include such things as flick-knives; it is unlawful to possess them and a prosecution will normally result if a person is found with one. Class 2 offensive weapons can be virtually anything – bricks, milk bottles, dustbin lids, hatpins, pepper-pots, or aerosols. With class 1 weapons, simple possession is sufficient to convict, but with class 2 weapons, intent has to be shown.

A woman may spray lacquer on her hair but she may not deliberately spray it in the eyes of another person with the intention of causing injury. A hatpin can be used to secure a hat, but it may not be used to stab someone. A bricklayer can handle bricks on a building site, but there is no lawful reason to take one, wrapped in a sock, to a football match.

Under no circumstances should a person carry any object with intent to use it as a weapon. In the past, women have been advised to carry a small pot of pepper, covered with a paper lid. There is no lawful reason for having such an item on the person, and anyone found in possession of it would be liable to prosecution.

An increasing number of prosecutions each year involve the rice flail. This consists of two wooden batons joined by chain or cord. In use, it is swung around and passed from hand to hand. In the hands of an expert the rice flail can be dangerous. It is known as a covert weapon, and its possession for the purposes of self defence is unlawful.

Although a weapon should be used in self defence only as a last resort, it is better to live through an attack and argue later about the defence used than to die or suffer serious injury.

The police should be notified of all assaults. If possible, the parties involved and the witnesses should remain at the scene of the incident. The attacker may be restrained until the police arrive and he can be handed into custody.

In conclusion:
>   Do not over-respond to an attack.
>   Do not bluff; make no threat unless you are prepared to carry it out.
>   Survive an attack and argue about it afterwards.

WEAPONS AND SELF DEFENCE

Before anyone contemplates using weapons in self defence, he should read the section on law. No weapon should ever be produced by the victim unless he is prepared to use it. The question of weapons is difficult; no reasonable person condones their use, but it must be reluctantly recognised that they may be necessary in life or death situations.

The problem is that the victim may wrongly assess the degree of personal danger. A householder may go downstairs in the dead of night, armed with a knife, to confront a burglar. Perhaps the burglar turns out to be a young and unarmed person against whom the householder could easily prevail. In the darkness, can the householder be sure that the burglar is young and unarmed? Can he chance throwing away his weapon and tackling the youngster, or will he be reluctant to let go of the weapon and perhaps be goaded into using it? On the other hand, is there more than one armed intruder lurking in the dark?

The safest thing to do is to lock the bedroom door and summon aid, either by dialling 999 or by shouting out of the window. If there are children in another bedroom, the correct course of action is to rush into their room and lock the door.

In the early hours of the morning the senses are sometimes unreliable, and the householder will be wary of summoning the police, with all that entails, to chase away a cat that has got into the kitchen and

WEAPONS AND SELF DEFENCE

knocked over some plates. If an intruder is suspected, the householder should switch on all the lights and, making as much noise as possible, go downstairs to find out the reason for the disturbance. If evidence of a burglar is seen, the police should be called. The householder should not try to tackle a burglar, who may be armed.

In describing the use of weapons by the victim, it is assumed that all other forms of self defence have been exhausted or are inapplicable, the victim honestly believes that he is in serious danger, and there is no possibility of running away. It is also assumed that the average person does not have caches of weapons stored about the house (even if he has, they may not be where they are actually needed). Weapons of opportunity must provide the victim's arsenal. These can be categorised as cutting/piercing, striking, or projectile weapons.

Cutting weapons are knives, found in any kitchen. Sharp carving knives and fruit knives are ideal because they are light and can be used dextrously, even by an inexperienced person. They should be concealed along the back of the forearm and, when the attacker comes close enough, jabbed into his upper leg. Initially they should not be displayed, since the attacker can pick up a chair, pin the victim against the wall, and take the knife away. Once the attacker has seen the knife and the element of surprise is lost, it should be held in the rear hand and carried close to the body.

A knife should be used to slash at the attacker's limbs, rather than at his face or body. Most people have a horror of being cut, and a couple of superficial but copiously bleeding wounds will drive away all but the most manic of attackers. Pointed knives with a blade length greater than two and a half inches should not be stabbed into the body, since they can kill.

Striking weapons should be short and heavy — a broom handle is of little use. They must have sufficient mass to develop force and yet be short enough to be used in enclosed spaces. The only household implements that spring to mind are pokers, rolling pins, and heavy frying pans. Baton weapons should

WEAPONS AND SELF DEFENCE

not be swung wildly, as this makes them easier to avoid and counter. They are better used to jab at the attacker's groin or face, as an extension of the normal first echelon hand weapons. (A first echelon response is intended to stop an attack. Techniques are described in Section 3.) A baton can be used as a club once the attacker is brought to his knees. It is less frightening than a knife, and the attacker may continue even if the victim produces a baton.

Weapons function as deterrents, letting the attacker know that the victim is not going to accept passively whatever is handed out. They may not worry the committed attacker but could dissuade the casual thug.

Projectile weapons include anything with enough mass to cause injury when they are thrown — solid objects, such as full milk bottles, plant pots, and chairs. They are used to make the attacker momentarily lose attention, thus giving the victim time to escape. A purse can be flung at the attacker, as can a cup of tea or a plate of food. A table can be overturned in his path, and chairs tipped up in an effort to slow his advance.

In the street, milk bottles, bricks, large stones, and dustbin lids can be pressed into service. A dustbin lid is very useful against an attacker with a knife, as it protects the hands and body against cuts.

If the attacker produces a weapon, the victim must evaluate the outcome of the attack. Armed attackers seem as likely to knife a co-operative victim as an unco-operative one, so response or otherwise is a matter of personal choice. It is assumed that any valuables have been handed over and the victim has tried to escape and failed.

The only defence against a knife attack is distance. The attacker will hold the knife in his rear hand and try to seize the victim with the free one, pulling him on to a thrust. The victim must try to keep out of range while avoiding being manoeuvred into a corner. If a knife attack takes place in a small area, such as a lift, the victim has no means of defence other than trying to catch and hold the knife bearing arm, at the same time biting, kicking, and clawing. Both parties are so close that any warding off of the knife arm can allow the victim to go directly in, hard at the attacker's eyes. Under these circumstances, the victim could, with justification, inflict severe damage.

Where there is more space, the victim should first withdraw as far as possible. He should ward off slashes with anything he can pick up. Tea towels, dish cloths, raincoats, jackets, cardigans, or shoes can be wrapped around the leading hand. In a real knife attack, the victim must expect to be cut. Any counter-attacks should be made with kicks, since shoes (especially leather ones) can give some protection.

The attacker may produce a sharpened screwdriver. This is a less frightening weapon than a knife, since it cannot be used to slash, but it is still potentially lethal. Great care must be taken to avoid being pulled on to it. Distance and timing are the best means of self defence in this instance.

Attacks with batons are slightly easier to deal with. Pick-axe handles and chains must be swung hard, and the victim can make use of the dead time (when the force of the attack is at its lowest) before and after each swipe. If he can get inside the swing, the force of the blow is lessened.

Firearms should never be challenged. The attacker can inflict fatal injuries from a distance, and even if he does close, it takes less effort to pull a trigger than it does to try a technique. Depending on the propellant charge and the type of shot used, a shotgun can kill at 40 yards. The concept of safe distance thus takes on a new meaning.

Attack by a number of assailants is very dangerous. There may be a case here for the victim using a weapon. Where two attackers are involved, the danger is not actually doubled, because unless they work closely as a team, there is always the possibility that one will get in the other's way. The victim must keep moving all the time and not become crowded into corners or against walls. At no time must he allow an attacker to get behind him. Only strikes can be used, since holds and throws take too long for an inexperienced person to apply. The victim cannot afford to wait for an attack; he must take the offensive. The theory is that the victim should feint at one attacker, then go for the eyes of the second, before returning to deal with the first.

In conclusion:
> Only take up a weapon as a last resort, but then be prepared to use it.
> Do not attempt self defence against a person armed with a weapon except as a last resort.

REALISM IN SELF DEFENCE

Many self defence courses are unrealistic in three respects. The first is an incorrectly envisaged attack, the second is an incorrect response to a counter-attack, and the third is an error of omission — what to do after the attack has been halted.

The first was mentioned in the introduction. Most people do not have to deal with violence on a regular basis, so they cannot be expected to know what form attacks actually take. Looking at the average self defence course, one sees rear strangles where the attacker is standing well back from the victim and using straight arms. This cannot be logical.

There is a whole series of escapes from straight armed single and double hand lapel grasps. A clever piece of leverage works against the straight elbow, prising the grasp loose and leading into a restraint hold. Unfortunately, lapel grasp is never done with straight arms because this approach would make it impossible for the attacker to hold the victim securely. These escape techniques are therefore of academic interest only.

Little emphasis seems to be laid on the really important aspects of self defence, such as evading an attack so it is rendered harmless. If the attacker manages to get close enough to grab hold, the first line of defence is crossed and subsequent options are severely reduced.

The second shortcoming — incorrect response to counter-attack — is less obvious. There are slick self defence displays involving whole series of brilliant techniques, one following the other without pause. The attacker grasps a lapel and is promptly kicked in the groin; immediately afterwards his arm is seized and a throw used to dump him subdued on the floor; for the *coup de grâce*, the defender follows down and applies a punishing lock. If, however, the opening technique fails, the entire following sequence collapses. The victim is promptly scooped up and dealt with.

It is not a good idea to embark on a sequence of moves which all depend on the effectiveness of the first. Flexibility must be maintained, and if the sequence should show signs of going wrong, it must be quickly aborted. Any sequence of techniques must take into account the outcome of each individually.

If an attacker is knocked unconscious or runs away, there is no problem of what to do next. On the other hand, a restraint hold is not an end in itself, but merely a way of holding someone captive until help arrives. Yet self defence courses seem to finish at that point, leaving the attacker and victim in a potentially dangerous stalemate.

If one considers attacks in a logical way, it is obvious that an unarmed attacker will try to close to where he can use his hands and feet. Once in range, he will strike and/or grab the victim in some way. The strike will be either a punch or a kick, and the grab may itself be a prelude to a punch, elbow, knee, or head butt. The grab firmly holds the victim while coercion – implied or physical – is applied.

The purpose of coercion is to cause injury or, in a sexual assault, to obtain physical co-operation. The attacker will try to intimidate the victim, perhaps by inflicting a painful injury right at the start. A punch in the face can break the nose or smash teeth, with attendant laceration of the lips and mouth. The victim thereafter loses all interest in counter-attacking and tries only to avoid further injury.

It is instructive to consider techniques used during an attack. A punch can be either circular or straight. Whichever it is, it will not be left out passively to be attacked. The effective circular punch occurs less frequently in fast flurries of blows because it uses a great deal of body movement in comparison with a straight jab.

A kick will be of the swinging variety and aimed at

the stomach, groin, knees, or shin. It has longer range than the punch and is more commonly used against men than women. A kick to the groin, stomach, or knee can collapse the victim, making him open to further attack.

There are various forms of grapples. Where the aim is to move the victim, he can be picked up bodily and carried to a car, dragged to a concealed spot by the arm, or simply thrown to the ground. A simple grab is made at a trailing arm and the smaller victim physically pulled along. If ineffective resistance is offered, the simple grab may be supplemented by a face punch (to intimidate) and/or changed to an arm or wrist twist. If the attacker has little physical superiority over the victim, an initial intimidating strike is logical. It is improbable that a man will be caught by an arm and dragged, but more likely that his arm will be twisted. The casual attacker will be unwilling to become involved in a wrestling match unless he is skilled at a martial art or combat sport. A quick and effective victory will be sought, or the attacker will withdraw and seek a more co-operative victim.

A strong attacker can use enough leverage on a joint to cause severe pain. It is as well to co-operate with someone applying this kind of technique since great skill is needed to escape without injury. An ineffective attempt may alert the attacker and lead to a fracture or dislocation. While the hold is being applied, the attacker can do little else, as his own body weapons are being fully used. When the hold is released in preparation for something else, there will be an opportunity for the victim to counter-attack more safely.

A strangle is a means of gaining rapid submission and, if kept on, results in unconsciousness or death. A single handed front strangle is always used to intimidate, perhaps to pin the head prior to a face punch. Except when employed by a strong attacker, it is not used to choke the victim. The applying arm is bent at the elbow and the victim is probably forced back against a wall or fence. A double handed strangle is also normally applied with bent elbows and is easily capable of choking the victim without further measures. It requires a lot of strength and is less likely to be used effectively with other techniques. The strangle should always be countered as early as possible since delay can result in the victim becoming unconscious.

The rear strangle is a common surprise attack. The forearm whips around the face from behind and the neck is caught between the forearm and biceps. Squeezing the front of the throat crushes the windpipe, and pressure on either side cuts off blood supply to the brain, causing rapid unconsciousness. Sometimes a reinforcing arm pushes the victim's head diagonally forwards, causing a neck fracture. The skilled attacker will pull the victim backwards off balance, making an effective counter more difficult.

The full nelson is a pinion hold. The attacker approaches from behind and brings his arms under the victim's armpits, lacing the fingers together at the back of the victim's neck. Tightening his grip forces the victim's head forward, causing severe pain.

The full nelson can be applied directly only by a skilled attacker to a weaker victim. It requires complicated movements and the victim can easily avoid it unless he is first distracted or stunned. Once it is applied, though, the average person cannot break free and the attacker can apply enough leverage to break the victim's neck or to force his head into a wall.

A single handed lapel grasp will probably be followed by a punch. A double handed grasp may lead on to a head butt or knee to the groin. It is difficult (but not impossible) to head-butt effectively when the victim is free to pull back; he must be pinioned effectively, and this requires both hands. A knee to the groin can be used from a one handed lapel grasp but, again, it is most effective when the victim is firmly held.

Headlocks are popular fighting techniques. The most common is the head chancery, in which the attacker's arm wraps around the victim's head and pulls it down to his hip. The neck is painfully wrenched and the head can be rammed into brick walls. A smaller person can be held single handed while the attacker's other hand punches to the face or attacks the eyes.

When assessing a potential attack, one should take note of the body weapons available to both the attacker and the victim, and the vulnerable targets within their reach. Thus, if the defender is caught in a rear strangle and must act quickly, it is pointless for him to consider a kick. His hands are free, however, and the only vulnerable target they can attack blind with any chance of success is the attacker's groin.

When someone is kicked in the groin, he does not freeze into immobility. He leans forwards, clutching his injured privates with both hands, or falls to the floor and assumes a semi-foetal position, with the head bowed and the knees drawn up. It is difficult and rather pointless to train someone to kick to the groin, then seize an extended arm and twist it. If the kick connects solidly with the groin, the wrist hold becomes superfluous.

When a punch is evaded, the attacker will not wait patiently for the victim to counter-attack. At the first inkling that the technique has missed, the attacker is already lining up for a follow-up and there is only the briefest of times in which to counter. If the counter is unsuccessful, it is useless for the victim to stay close and trade techniques with a larger attacker. It is better to move back out of range and wait for another opportunity. The defender must always try to obtain the advantage.

A wrist hold can go horribly wrong if the attacker is not successfully distracted. A light flick to the groin causes a momentary distraction and if the follow-up hold is successfully applied at that moment, all is well. If the kick catches the thigh instead of the groin, going for a wrist hold could take the defender on to a punch in the head. The key is the strike/distraction; this must be seen to work before the sequence is continued.

A strong person can sometimes withstand a surprisingly heavy blow without hesitating. A strong elbow into the attacker's solar plexus may provoke no reaction at all, not even a grunt. Stamping on his feet may simply make him angry. It is wrong to assume that a strong blow will automatically have a significant effect, so there should be a brief hesitation before plunging in with a follow-up.

It is not sensible for a weaker victim to hold a strong attacker in a restraint hold. The strong victim can use a restraint hold successfully and have a reserve of power, but a small victim will find his technical ability balanced by the attacker's greater strength — a situation that will not wait long to be resolved. It is theoretically possible to march the erstwhile attacker to a police station (assuming it is not too far away), or to shout for help, but passers-by may be confused about who is the aggressor and who is the victim and may decide to intervene wrongly. The noise may also attract the attacker's friends.

The stronger victim can increase leverage on a joint until the attacker's arm or wrist is fractured, but few people are mentally capable of this. It does, however, have the advantage of putting the attacker out of action. Another way out of the impasse is to make the attacker promise to behave himself, then release him. In this case, however, the victim is likely to find the promise quickly forgotten and a wiser and more cautious attacker squaring up for a second try.

A restraint hold should be used only by a stronger person, and then only if help is likely to be on hand and it is not appropriate to stun the attacker and escape.

In conclusion:
   Look for realism in practice.
   The techniques used should really work.

ASSERTION

Not all attacks involve outright violence from the start. Some begin gradually, and it may be possible to head off violence by adopting a positive attitude. Animals will often turn on a weaker member of the group, and so, it seems, do some humans. The bully is a coward at heart, deliberately choosing victims he thinks will submit. He is not always right in his choice, however, and there are numerous cases of

ASSERTION

bullies being put to flight by their intended victims.

Size is no measure of self defence ability. Some small people are quite clearly unsuitable material for any bully, no matter how big he is. Conversely, there are large and athletic individuals who give an impression of being obvious prey. In both cases, it is not words but attitude and body language which convey the message.

Some people adopt – or have imposed on them – a dominant or a submissive role. Dominance is encouraged by self esteem. People with low self esteem appear submissive and easily dominated, adopting body postures which make them targets for aggression from the more dominant. The most obvious of these is the eye encounter. The dominant person tends to look people directly in the eye, searching for the sudden look-away that breaks eye contact and indicates submission.

The dominant person tries to appear taller, perhaps by standing over someone who is sitting. He may encroach upon someone else's personal space, by draping an arm round his shoulders, for instance. The submissive person may feel uncomfortable but will be unable to express this by clear signals. A submissive woman who does not want to be touched will tell the man 'not to do that', but she will smile, almost apologetically, as she says it, thus providing a conflicting signal. On one hand, she is making a statement; on the other, she is smiling as though to say she does not really mean it. The signal is thus confused and can be misinterpreted, leading to a possible escalation of the situation, and perhaps ending with the man claiming he was encouraged.

The submissive self defence student should be aware of the danger of being taken as a target for aggression. The first step in avoiding this is to develop a reasonable level of self esteem. This should not be founded on wealth, sex, or skin colour, but on appreciation of qualities of character. Self awareness must be cultivated because with it comes acceptance of one's own faults and recognition of one's good points. It is necessary both to develop and to refer to a strong ego.

There is no reason why any person should submit

to another, except voluntarily. A proper sense of self respect will demand that action be taken to avoid being imposed on. Someone trying to press an unwanted extra drink will be told politely but firmly that it is not wanted.

People do not listen to themselves speaking. If they did, they might be disappointed. Is the voice squeaky and high-pitched under stress? Is it panicky and unsure? The voice is particularly important when signalling dominance or submissiveness. It should be strong without being loud, and should convey an impression of firmness. It should not rise in pitch, but should maintain an even tone and volume. Bluster is recognised as such and fools no one.

When one is speaking, the eyes should always be full on the person being spoken to and facial expressions should match the words being said. 'No' is said firmly and with a serious face, not with a nervous giggle which belies its meaning. The hands should not flutter about nervously, nor should they fold across the chest as though forming a barrier.

The stance should be upright, with the head held high. When one is expressing a firm viewpoint, the body should turn square on to the other person. Half turning can indicate a lack of confidence. When addressing someone who is standing, stand up also, so as not to be towered over. The back is kept straight when walking and the shoulders are thrown back. The head is held high and the eyes take in the surroundings. The step is firm and the stride vigorous.

Practising effective self assertion will mean that a bully will be less likely to see one as a potential victim.

In conclusion:
Cultivate self esteem.
Refuse to be dominated.
Ensure that this refusal is clear.

AWARENESS AND AVOIDANCE

Theory

Awareness is a state of mind – of knowing what is happening or may happen by gathering all the available facts and interpreting them correctly. The aware car driver sees stoplights ahead, notes the wet road surface, and interprets those facts before taking action and slowing down. There is both conscious and unconscious awareness; one requires an effort of mind, the other is an undemanding habit. The latter is developed through practice at listening and observing until, like the conditioned reflexes necessary for a physical self defence response to an attack, it becomes completely automatic.

Quite complicated activities can take place without conscious direction once a habit has been created. The learner driver, for example, concentrating on how to change gear, forgets to steer the car. The accomplished driver can concentrate on steering the car out of the way of obstacles while he changes gear without consciously thinking about it.

Concentration involves a conscious effort during which awareness is narrowed to deal with one thing to the detriment of others. For example, when one is threading a needle, the senses – let alone the hands – concentrate on that task to such an extent that it would be impossible to drive a car at the same time. Prolonged concentration quickly causes fatigue and consequent lapses. Awareness as a part of a self defence system must be maintained on as high an unconscious level as possible, so it can be sustained without effort. To achieve this, it must remain unconcentrated.

When the possibility of danger is detected, it is very difficult not to concentrate on it to the exclusion of everything else. Perhaps an attacker is struggling in a restraint hold and concentration is devoted to keeping him immobile. This narrowing of awareness can mean that the arrival of the attacker's friends goes unnoticed until it is too late.

Awareness training is an important part of combat

AWARENESS AND AVOIDANCE

sports and martial art training. One of many oriental expressions describing it is: 'The mind must be like a lake – reflecting what is around it, yet having no form of itself.' It was an integral part of the training of Japanese warriors who were taught never to be caught unawares. They learnt to sit in a way that made it possible to get up quickly, draw a weapon, and counter-attack. Where they sat was also important; it should be facing the door. Whenever they sat down the first thing they did was to mark out in their minds an escape route to be taken in case of an emergency. A modern samurai will still sit by the door in a bus, aeroplane, or train. In a restaurant he always holds his cup of *cha* (tea) high so it can be dashed in the face of a would-be attacker.

The need for awareness is not new, nor is it restricted to the Orient. The Bible too has something to say about it. When Gideon was choosing his troops to fight the Midianites, God told him to watch the men as they drank. 'Leave behind,' said God, 'those who lower their faces to the water to drink and take only those who raise the water to their lips in cupped hands. These are all you will need.' (Judg 7:5–7.)

Awareness is thus a vital part in any self defence system. The student trains himself to notice more things about the environment with a view to detect-

ing areas of possible risk. After a while this becomes automatic and the conscious mind no longer concentrates on it. Awareness of risks will lead to positive steps to avoid them. The trick is to be as aware as possible without becoming paranoid.

Avoidance is the practical application of awareness. Successful self defence lies in avoiding trouble and high-risk situations. It is better to be aware of and avoid trouble than to meet it head on, relying upon a physical self defence response. The aware person stands more chance of avoiding danger or quickly extricating himself from it.

Playing safe
At parties, drinking too much alcohol should be avoided unless a trusted and sober car-owning friend is at hand. Alcohol reduces awareness and makes risks more difficult to avoid. A solitary drunk is at the mercy of any would-be assailant. Strangers who have had too much to drink should be avoided since they are sometimes unpredictable and can become violent without apparent reason.

The solitary car driver must be aware of risk when he stops late at night at traffic lights in an unsavoury area. An unlocked front door can result in him being dragged on to the pavement. An unlocked back door

Be aware of areas of potential danger

AWARENESS AND AVOIDANCE

Walking close in gives no indication of what could be lurking in a doorway

Walking away from the wall can give a better view

AWARENESS AND AVOIDANCE

can admit unwelcome guests. These risks can be avoided by locking all doors and closing all windows.

Hitch-hikers are at risk each time they accept a lift from a stranger. The risk multiplies when there is more than one person in the car. No really aware person would accept a lift in a car containing several men. Conversely, there is a risk every time a driver gives a lift to a stranger. Appearance is nothing to go on. Giving a lift to more than one stranger is foolhardy.

The aware person will know of the risks that may be lurking in darkened shop doorways, alley fronts, or just around the corner late at night. The risk of being suddenly surprised can be avoided if one walks on the outside third of the pavement, crosses the road, or (if there is no traffic) walks in the road. From these positions, the angle of sight is altered so there is an earlier view into dark corners.

It is a widely held misapprehension that wearing brief or revealing clothes means the wearer is promiscuous. Any woman walking home late at night might attract unwelcome attention, but if she is scantily dressed the risk is increased. If she cannot avoid being out of doors late at night, risk should be reduced by wearing a coat to cover up party clothes.

There are also risks in travelling on public transport. Bus and train stations can be dangerous places, but risk may be reduced by standing close to a manned office, or with a mixed-sex group of people. Where there are no crowds, one should wait in an illuminated area.

Noisy gangs of people should be avoided, if necessary by crossing the road. No attempt should be made to go to a train platform or bus pier in the middle of such a crowd. If the gang comes along subsequently, risk can be marginally reduced by standing next to people already quietly waiting.

When the train pulls in, the aware person will avoid entering or remaining in an empty carriage. Anyone can get in afterwards. There is less risk in choosing a carriage containing a sprinkling of people and taking a seat near the door. The aware person sits only in the downstairs cabin of a bus; on single-manned vehicles, that seat should be as near the driver as possible.

Having arrived at his destination, the aware person will not stand around in the dark waiting to be collected. A telephone call made in advance will ensure that a lift is ready at a previously agreed well lit spot. If waiting is unavoidable, one should choose a manned ticket hall or anywhere with separate groups of people, such as a pub, fast-food shop, or minicab office.

A person alone in a house must make sure all the doors are locked and windows closed. Unexpected callers should be treated with caution and their identities established before admitting them. This can be done by means of a spyhole and porch light. A security chain on the door will allow small items to be passed through, but it must be screwed firmly into the frame of the door and be strong enough to withstand a sudden shoulder charge or kick. Only the front door should be opened at night; callers to the rear of the house should be told to go round to the front.

Porches should be well illuminated, and panelled with clear glass so that any activity can be seen from the road. The front door should be of solid wood for most of its construction, and capable of being locked with a mortise or deadlock.

An attack alarm can give some protection from risk. Two types are available, the portable and the installed. The portable slips into a pocket (not a handbag) and, when activated, gives out a penetrating shriek that may distract the casual would-be attacker by drawing attention to his activities. The type selected must, once it is activated, sound continuously until its gas reservoir is used up. This can prove embarrassing, but it is better to be embarrassed than injured. The portable attack alarm suffers from the disadvantage that it can be put out of action or muffled by the persistent attacker.

Installed attack alarms in houses are normally part of an intruder detection system. They take the form of wall mounted boxes with a push button on the top. When the button is pressed, the alarm is set off. The alarm should, ideally, have both an internal and an external self-powered noisemaker which cannot be reached to damage it. The alarm is switched off by means of a key hidden somewhere about the house. Installed attack alarms should be sited near the front door and in a designated safe room. The safe room is generally a bedroom selected for its strong door secured by a good deadlock and perhaps rack bolts too. There should be a telephone extension in the room.

In conclusion
Despite all reasonable awareness and avoidance, there will always be an element of risk. When one is faced with a potential attack, a physical response should still be avoided if at all possible.

If the attacker is after money, it should be handed over without hesitation. It is always better to lose money than health. The aware person out at night will always separate valuables and carry them in different places. A small amount of money can be left in the handbag or wallet and given up when the victim is threatened. Throwing it to the ground and running away can be considered.

A casual – that is, unpremeditated – sex attacker can sometimes be deterred through remorse. The aware victim will try to provoke feelings of guilt or sympathy and will offer no resistance at the encounter stage. She will try to chat in a friendly manner, showing concern for the attacker and his frame of mind. The aim is to convince him that he is really a nice man and does not want to hurt her. This tactic has worked, and must be seriously considered.

The premeditated sex attacker has selected his victim with care, ensuring that the surroundings are suitable to his purposes. He will not be deterred by words and may become excited at the sight of tears or pleading. To the sadistic attacker, the sex act itself may be of less importance than the attendant pain and humiliation inflicted upon the victim. A token physical resistance on the part of the victim may prove an incentive for the attacker to increase the level of violence used; paradoxically, no response at all may provoke the same excess.

AWARENESS AND AVOIDANCE

The aware person will note the attitude of the attacker. A red face and blustering manner hold less danger than a pale face and quiet approach. With the latter, threats and shouts are unnecessary because a mental commitment to violence has already been made.

When faced with a potential assault, one should make every possible effort to avoid violence. In any fight there is a possibility of serious injury, and prosecutions will surely follow. It is far better to swallow insults and make apologies, even when they are unwarranted. Such actions are the mark of a strong person, acting from a position of strength.

When all other ways have been tried and a physical response is inevitable, the victim must make a total commitment to it if there is to be any chance of success at all.

In conclusion:
Be aware of potential risks.
Take steps to avoid them.

SECTION 2 PRACTICAL (1) BASIC TECHNIQUES

TIMING

Expressed simply, timing is knowing when to respond to an attack and, conversely, when not to. The aim is to counter-attack to a vulnerable target when the opponent is incapable of retaliating. In some situations the opportunity for a counter-attack is strictly limited, and at such times a knowledge of timing is invaluable. The best counter-attack in the world will fail if the timing is wrong.

The attack, when it comes, can take any one of a number of forms and the defender cannot be expected to anticipate which will be used. Timing provides a breathing space during which the attack can be channelled into familiar pathways and dealt with.

A powerful man may lift up and bodily carry a woman to a place of concealment. While being

It is not possible to make an effective self defence technique from this position

TIMING

Never stand square on to a potential attack

Try to maintain a safe distance and effective guard

carried she can certainly struggle violently, but there are no vulnerable targets she can reach with sufficient force or accuracy. Her response is limited to making herself as awkward to hold on to as possible. A knowledge of timing teaches her that in this situation it is best to delay a self defence response until she has been set down.

Similarly, it is not a good time to try a self defence technique when a knife is being held to one's throat. It is better to wait for the attacker to become pre-occupied with something else before one responds.

A tactical use of timing is demonstrated by the following example. The attacker grabs the female victim by her shoulder. Instead of trying to pull free, she steps forward into his embrace, keeping her arms low and slightly forward, taking care to appear relaxed and co-operative. As she is gathered in, she seizes the crutch of his trousers in a tight grip, effectively diverting his mind from his original purpose.

It is best to respond to an attacker's technique just as it is starting or immediately after it has missed. In the split second before someone is about to throw a strong punch or kick, the eyes momentarily narrow. This can be confirmed by closely watching a partner's face as he suddenly attacks. The momentary squint gives just enough warning for evasive action

TIMING

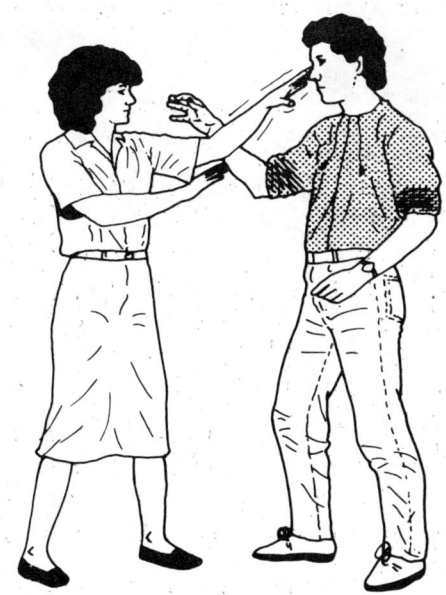

Countering the attacker's technique before it has a chance to develop

to be taken. To practise it, the attacker should suddenly lunge forwards while the defender side-steps. The aim is to prevent the reaching arms from making contact. The squint will not appear if an attack is made without power, as it would be in the case of a feint.

The attacker's strike begins from a stationary position, accelerates to the target, and loses speed as it is retrieved to be used again. It is travelling with maximum power when the target distance is reached, and that is when it is most difficult to block or avoid. The reflex squint beforehand allows the defender to anticipate the blow, moving away from it or even countering during the early stage when it has yet to build up energy. This early stage is known as dead time. The attacker will be concentrating on launching the blow and a sudden counter at that time will cause confusion and loss of composure. Dead time can be exploited for countering kicks, punches, and grabs.

If, by successful evasion, the technique is made to miss, there will be a short time during which energy is shed before being retrieved for further use. This, too, is dead time and may be exploited. A good example is when a heavy man throws a powerful swinging punch. If it misses, he spins as though to

TIMING

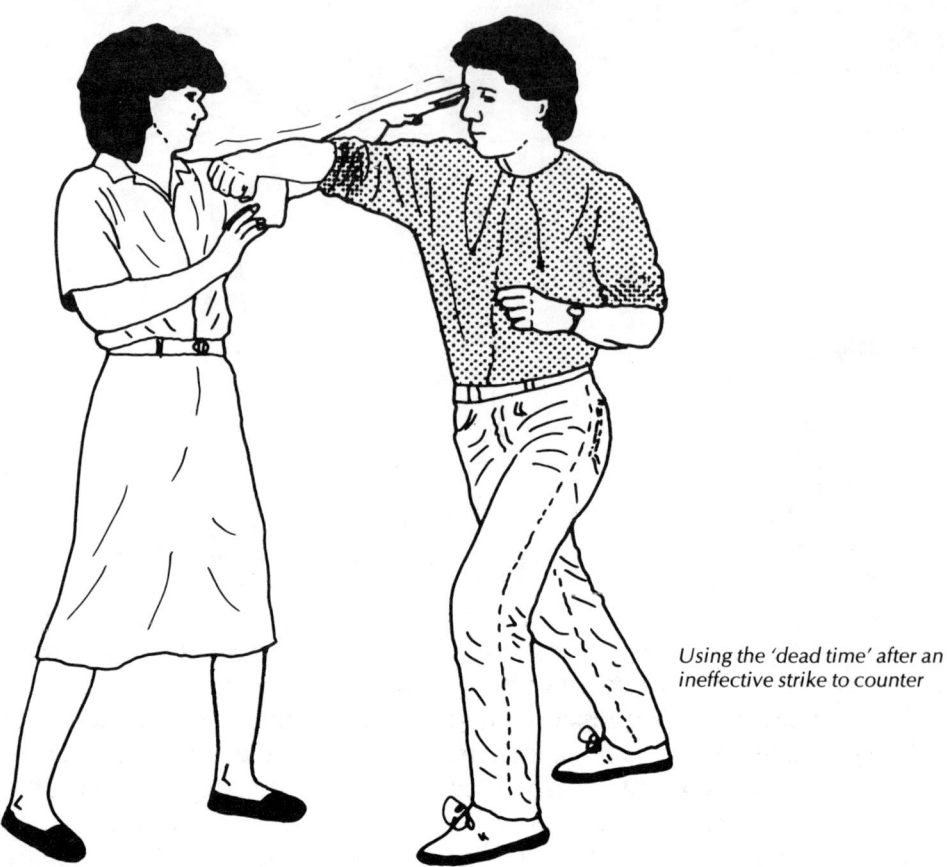

Using the 'dead time' after an ineffective strike to counter

follow it and, in extreme cases, falls over. Between the technique missing and being retrieved, no further effective attack can be delivered.

This can be practised with a partner swinging long but slow circling punches at the defender's head. The defender leans back slightly to avoid them before quickly moving in to counter. The counter used is not important during timing practice, when it should take the form of a gentle strike, making very light contact with the attacker's vulnerable points.

Great care must be taken when using dead time counters to an experienced fighter throwing straight, jabbing punches. Jabs do not have much commitment in their delivery and can be retrieved extremely quickly. A jabbing punch to the victim's face may form part of a co-ordinated one/two delivery. Attempting to move in quickly during the imagined dead time following the first jab will run the defender on to the second punch. For this reason, the MAC course begins all counter-attacks with a move away which makes safe.

In conclusion:
   Counter in the dead time before a technique picks up force.
   Counter in the dead time after a technique misses.
   Use timing to make safe.

BLOCKS AND EVASIONS

An attack is usually aimed at a target: a grasp is made to the lapel, a punch to the face, or a knee into the groin. In all cases, the target is selected and a technique aimed at it. The idea in blocking is to interrupt the technique before it reaches its target. This can be achieved by knocking it off course. A jab to the face can be deflected to the side with the flat of the hand. As the technique comes in, the defender leans back, putting weight on the rear leg and smacking the punch off target. During this block, the forearm must be held vertical and the fingers stiffened on impact. Any variation in height of the incoming technique can be taken on the forearm between wrist and elbow.

A grab for the throat can be deflected the same way. Alternatively, both arms can rise upwards and across the front of the body so they cross at the wrists. The grab gets caught between them and can be deflected to one side or the other. Kicks can be scooped to one side using an underhand parry that catches the side of the calf with the muscle of the forearm, or batted away by swinging down the raised forearm across the body. Regardless of the block used, the aim is to deflect the incoming technique rather than meet it full on, force against force.

Head block is useful for demonstrating the principle of deflection. To make it interesting, the partner can use a broomstick held in both hands to hit the defender lightly, square on the head. The attack is performed slowly and without force but, as the principles are learned, it can be gradually speeded

BLOCKS AND EVASIONS

up. The defender extends the leading arm diagonally upwards and obliquely towards the descending blow. The blocking arm is rotated, palm upwards, so the stick catches it about wrist level. The inclined forearm acts as a runner along which the descending stick travels, deflecting the blow to the side and missing the head altogether.

The block is made safer if the defender steps forward to meet the blow, closing range and robbing the stick of its power. The blocking arm must be at virtually the same angle as the blow if it is to be deflected without pain. The head must be kept below the top of the blocking forearm or it will interrupt the smooth deflection.

The principles of leverage can be applied to a block so that minimum force can produce maximum effect. The attacking limb must be blocked at its extremity – the arm at the wrist, the leg at the

Evading the attack

BLOCKS AND EVASIONS

lower calf or ankle. This will turn away, with little effort, even a very powerful blow.

To demonstrate the use of leverage, the partner extends an arm, holding it rigidly out with the elbow locked. The defender places his palm against the attacker's elbow and, using steady pressure, tries to deflect the arm. The partner should resist the deflection. The palm is next placed against the wrist and the same pressure applied. This time less effort will be needed to deflect the arm.

Deflecting close to the target is always a risky business. If the block is unsuccessful, the attacker's technique lands where he intended. For this reason, some schools of self defence advise stopping the technique further away, before it has gathered force. This is a good idea for technically competent people, but it requires timing and strength.

A swinging punch from a large man carries con-

Blocking an attack

BLOCKS AND EVASIONS

siderable force. Even if it is blocked successfully, it can still knock the defender off balance or at least hurt the blocking arm. A kick also contains a great deal of energy. If the block is not timed correctly, there is a chance of a fractured wrist or dislocated fingers. If distance has not been closed, a descending blow may cause serious bruising to the blocking arm.

Some blocks are specific and only work against a particular attack. A descending blow to the head cannot be deflected with a slapping block, and that block is also useless against a swinging punch to the face. Depending on which way the swing comes in, either it will curve around the block and go on into the target, or the block will be travelling the wrong way to stop it.

The person who depends on blocks must therefore correctly anticipate each attack, get the distance right, and be in the correct stance, ready to use the right block. This requires a degree of skill that is reached only after many years of practice. With this in mind, the originators of the MAC course have selected only two blocks, but between them they cover a wide range of self defence applications.

The first block is very effective against straight attacks to the face or chest. As the attack begins, the defender shifts to the side with the front leg and twists the hips so the body turns obliquely towards the attacker. The leading hand is pushed out, deflecting the attack with the palm. The fingers are held open and slightly curled, so the attacker's arm can be quickly grasped if need be. The sidestep and hip twist make the attack miss and the block is merely a guard.

The second is the cross block, effective against descending strikes to the head, swinging punches, and straight jabs to the face. This block too is used with a body movement. The defender steps back, taking the target out of range. If there is insufficient space to step back, weight is put on the rear leg. The body moves back and is kept upright with the face pulled back for safety. The elbows stay close to the sides and both arms move upwards and across the body, with fingers extended and palms towards the chest.

BLOCKS AND EVASIONS

Even when only half formed, the cross block can be partially effective because the crossed arms form a shield in front of the body. The block is completed when the arms move diagonally upwards towards the attacker and the palms rotate outwards. By swivelling the hips, the defender can meet a swinging punch, or deflect a descending blow to the side.

The body movement used in both blocks is very important. It is wrong to stand rooted to the spot in any self defence situation. Rapid movements are called for, taking the head and body away from the direction of attack. Because the attack is aimed at a target, movement of that target by even a couple of inches can cause it to miss. The block becomes merely a safety measure and if it fails, no harm is done.

This important principle of movement to avoid a blow is known as evasion. Evasion needs no physical strength, only a degree of co-ordination and agility. It is far better to evade an attack than to stand still and try to block it.

Whether evasion or blocks are used, unless the distance between attacker and defender is correct neither will work properly. The value of correct distancing is illustrated in the legend of the kung fu style called 'white stork'. It is said that a Shaolin Buddhist monk witnessed a fight between a stork and a bear. He noticed how the stork very wisely kept itself away from the bear's teeth and claws, darting in with its long beak whenever it was safe to do so. The bear could have killed the stork very easily but was kept from doing so by the latter's use of distance and evasion.

Evasive movements can be made in any direction. It is possible to step towards the attacker or to draw back from him. A sidestep or angled move is also effective. A simple evasion and counter can be practised by standing with the left foot forwards and facing a partner in similar stance. The partner aims a kick off the right foot into the groin; this is avoided by the defender moving diagonally outwards on the front foot. The outward movement takes the body clear of the kick and the forward component brings the defender close to the attacker. An elbow strike to the attacker's face is made all the more effective because both attacker and defender are moving towards each other as it lands (though the kick has been avoided).

While the kick is in progress, it is not possible for the partner suddenly to switch to something else. The kicking leg has to touch down before an effective follow-up can be used. Timing is important, and the counter-attack must be delivered while the partner is in mid-kick. Awareness also plays an important role, starting off the counter-attack at the earliest possible time. As the partner's eyes narrow in preparation for attack, the defender should be ready to move.

Another way to practise evasion is to have the partner aim slow punches or grabs to the head and body. The defender tries to evade by sidestepping and twisting the hips to face the attack obliquely, or by stepping back from it. A high blow can be ducked, but this particular evasion should be avoided because there is always a risk of follow-up strikes catching the defender's head while he is in an awkward, crouched position.

An attack has only to miss by an inch or so for the evasion to work. There is therefore a minimum effective distance for it. If the miss is by a small margin, the defender is left close to the attacker and in a good position to use dead time to deliver a counter-attack. If the defender moves well away with the evasion, it will not be possible to close quickly enough to take the advantage.

The defender should try to stay as close as possible to the attacker, to make use of any opportunities which may present themselves. Distance should be maintained so that an attack is easily evaded and the counter ready to use.

Evasions, like blocks, can be specific. It is important to identify the attack correctly and respond to it properly. A straight punch or grasp can be evaded by stepping to either side or by pulling back. Stepping sideways into the path of a swinging punch can be dangerous. Ducking to avoid a knee to the groin is another example of an incorrect evasion. When one is in doubt, it is always better to step back.

In conclusion:
> Evasions and blocks should be used together.
> When in doubt, move back and make safe.
> Maintain distance at all times.

BODY WEAPONS AND TARGETS

In unarmed self defence, the body itself provides the weapons to defeat the attacker. The most obvious weapon is the front fist, where the fingers are rolled down until their tips contact the pad of flesh running across the hand at their bases. By resting the fingertips on this pad, the fist is stiffened and made more solid in the same way that rolling it around a piece of dowelling can. To complete the fist, the fingers fold forward and the thumb bends across to lock them. It is important to keep the thumb on the outside of the fingers if it is not to be dislocated on impact. The thumb must not point forwards, otherwise it can catch in sleeves and clothing.

The knuckles are made to protrude by pulling back the bent fingers as far as possible. Only the knuckles, not the finger joints, make contact with the target. The shape of the fists can be improved by pressing them against a flat surface, such as a table top. With a little practice, it soon becomes possible to close a fist quickly just before impact.

Impact is made only with the two largest knuckles, because force is more effective when concentrated into a small area. To illustrate the point: if the palm of the hand is pressed against the chest, no discomfort is caused; if the same pressure is applied but through a braced fingertip, discomfort will be felt.

For the punch to be effective, it must efficiently transmit its kinetic energy (that possessed by a moving body) into the target. The arm must become rigid at the moment of impact and the wrist must be so angled as to give a straight line of bones from the knuckles, through the wrist, and direct to the bones of the forearm. By this means, the recipient is thumped with the equivalent of a pole, rather than a fist alone. The wrist angle is critical. If it is wrong, it causes the wrist to flex on impact, producing a sprain or fracture. This is why an impact pad should be used in training.

The knuckles, which are covered with only a thin layer of skin, can easily be cut or bruised. Martial artists develop them as weapons by hitting a punching post until thick layers of callus build up to protect the delicate bones and joints. For self defence purposes, the front fist is not a weapon of choice; the hammerfist is safer.

The hammerfist uses the closed fist formed in the manner described above, but strikes are made with a clubbing motion. The fist is raised above the head and the elbow well bent. It is swung downwards and on to the target, striking with the pad of flesh that is raised below the little finger. The tighter the fist, the bigger the pad. Extra force may be generated by using a focused impact (when the body is rigid) and bending the knees slightly, so body weight lends itself to the strike. It is important to land on the pad and not on the wrist.

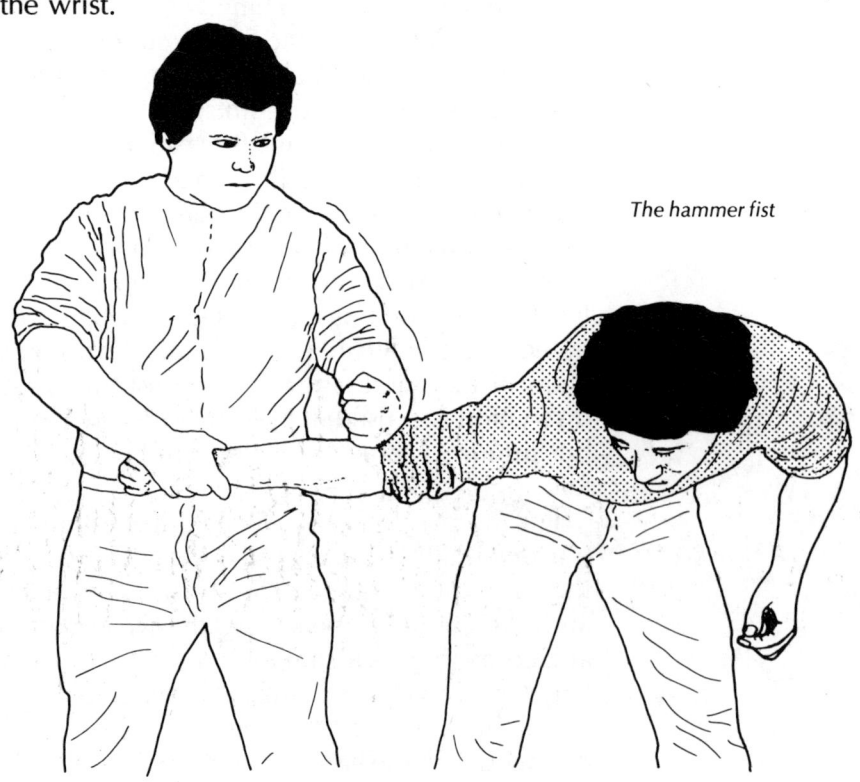

The hammer fist

If the fist is partially uncurled, the fingers and thumb become like a claw. Claw hand is useful for low energy strikes to the face, where the hooking fingers catch in eye sockets and cheeks. On contact, the fingers dig in, as though trying to grasp hold. Long fingernails can cause painful lacerations. To get the weapon quickly to the target, the relaxed hand is thrown at the face as though it were a ball. Claw hand can also be placed on the target.

Straightening the fingers a little more allows palm heel strike to be used. The base of the palm is well padded and there is little chance of damage to the bone. The fact that the wrist is not involved means it cannot bend during impact. Palm heel is used as a safer alternative to reverse or snap punch.

If the fingers are opened still further, with the wrist relaxed, they can be flicked across the eyes, producing an uncontrollable reflex blink. It is important they are kept relaxed, otherwise serious damage can be caused. The technique is delivered with a shaking movement of the elbow and wrist, as though shedding water from the fingers.

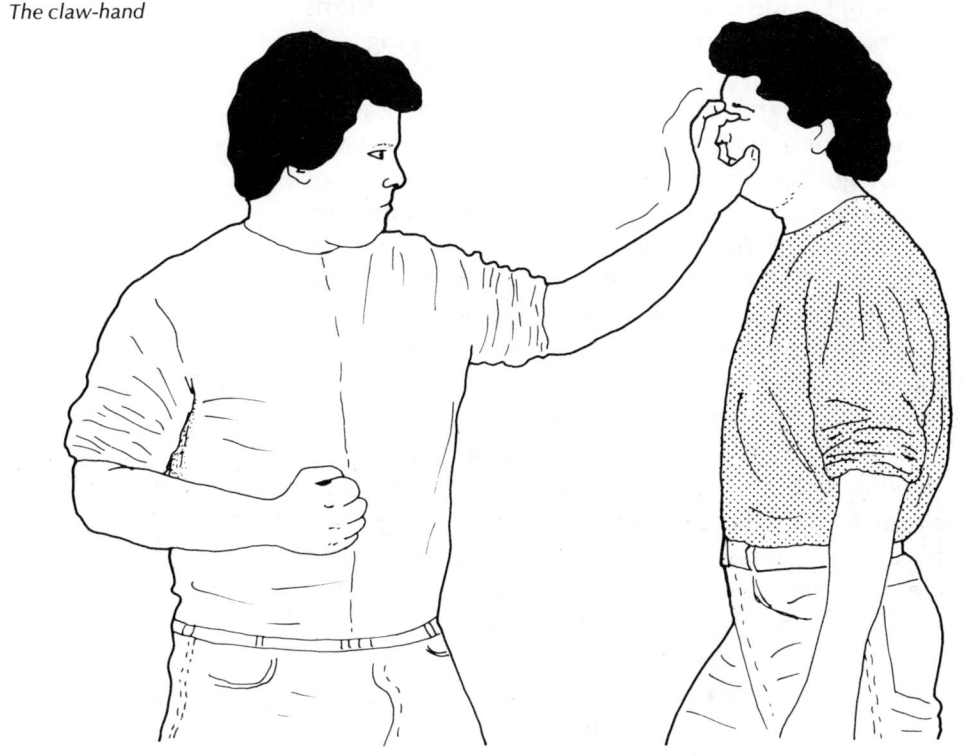

The claw-hand

BODY WEAPONS AND TARGETS

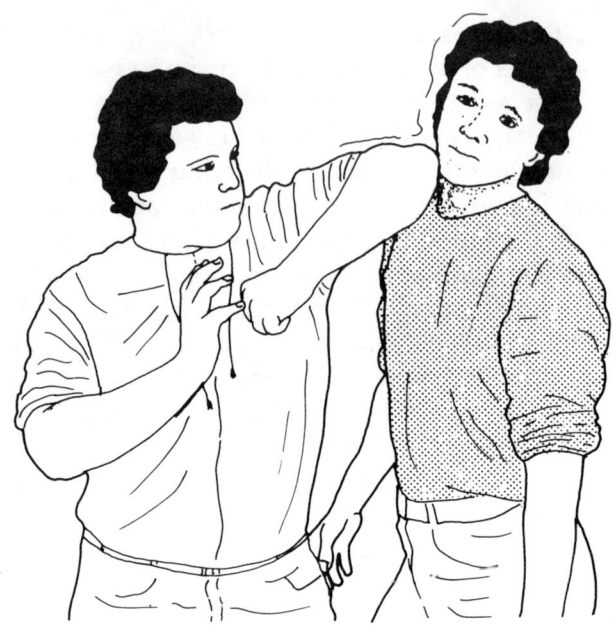

The elbow strike

The elbow is a good weapon, though it may bruise on hard impact. The trick is to keep the funny bone out of the way by making a fist and turning the little-finger side downwards. There are three forms of elbow strike – front, back, and descending.

Front elbow strike can be performed from a left stance, using the right elbow. The movement is the same as for a reverse punch – the hips twisting and weight going on to the front leg while the elbow rises and circles across the front of the body. On impact, the elbow is furthest away from the body and the forearm pulled well back. It is important to concentrate impact force at the tip of the elbow; a forearm smash is not nearly so effective. If body weight is thrown behind elbow strike, it becomes one of the most powerful of the arm weapons.

Back elbow is useful for dealing with an attacker standing behind. The open right hand stretches forwards as though to shake hands and the right leg steps quickly backwards at the same time. The length of the step depends on where the attacker is standing. If the step is too short, the rear elbow will not reach; if it is too long, the defender crashes into the attacker. Once the right foot settles, body weight is transferred on to it. The right knee bends and the

BODY WEAPONS AND TARGETS

hip turns slightly towards the attacker. The extended hand jerks back and the fingers close into a tight fist on impact. The whole move is timed so the elbow lands just as full weight comes down on to the back leg.

Descending elbow uses a downwards strike. From left stance, the open right hand extends vertically upwards. As the strike begins, the arm is sharply pulled down. On impact, the fist closes tightly and the knees bend, lending body weight to the impact. If focus is used, the technique becomes very strong.

Kicks have longer range and are more powerful than punches. Someone in punching range should not attempt to kick. The impact areas of the foot are the sole, the heel, the ball, the outside edge, and the instep. The instep, like the knuckles, is prone to bruising and care should be taken to target it only on

The groin kick

soft areas. The toes curl slightly downwards and the ankle is stiffened on impact. The foot should not be left loose, or injury will result.

The ball of the foot is a potent weapon because it concentrates considerable force over a small yet padded area. It is, however, difficult to use. The toes must be pulled upwards and back out of harm's way and the instep must form a straight line with the shin. This alignment can be seen by standing with the heel as high off the floor as possible. With shoes on, it is sometimes difficult to pull the toes right back; in this case they are withdrawn as far as possible and the kick is delivered with the heel low.

Dropping the heel still further allows impact to be made with the sole of the foot. The foot can be held toes upwards, or angled to the side when one is attacking such targets as the kneecap. The kick is driven out like a piston.

The heel may also be used to stamp at the kneecap. To practise this technique, an upright stance with the feet a shoulder-width apart is adopted. The upper body leans away from the direction of the kick and the knee of the kicking leg is raised. The leg is driven out and down and the bent supporting leg rotates, the heel swinging out in the same direction as the kick. To increase power, there is a slight drag forwards of the supporting leg. The kicking foot has the heel furthest out, the sole parallel to the floor, and the big toe slightly raised. The smaller toes are all turned down.

The heel is also used in the back kick. From left stance, the front knee is lifted up and brought back. The body leans forwards, the back arches, and the foot is driven backwards into the attacker's groin. The elbows are kept tight to the body and the head looks back over the left shoulder.

The knee is an effective close quarter weapon which can be used in two ways. From left stance, the victim seizes the attacker's head and pulls it down. The right leg swings forwards and up into the groin or face. To make it more powerful, the kicking foot points at the floor and the back is arched. The supporting leg straightens on impact.

The second way is facing the attacker in left

BODY WEAPONS AND TARGETS

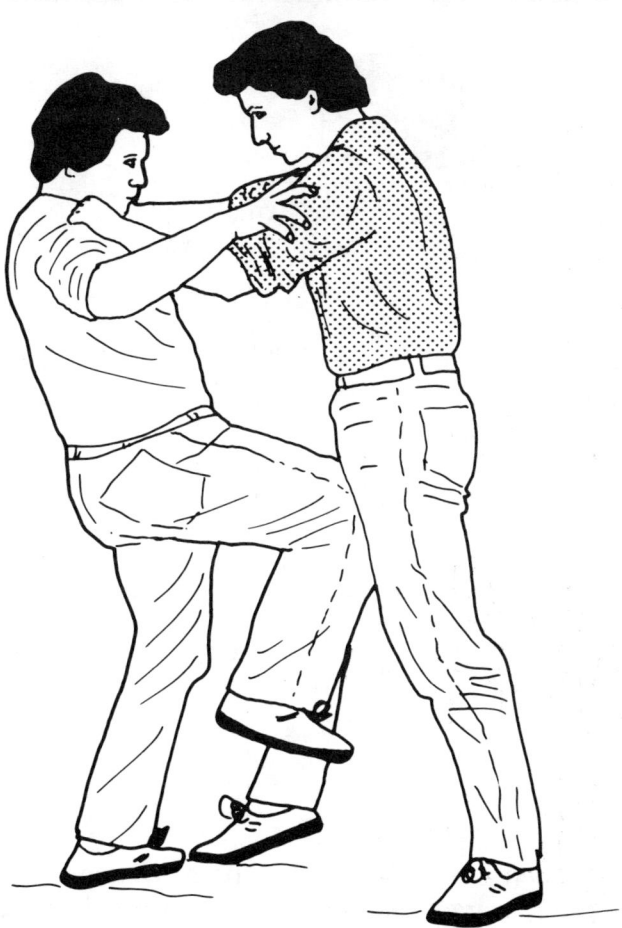

The knee

stance, but standing slightly to his right. The right arm reaches forward and hooks around the back of the attacker's neck, pulling his head down. The right knee lifts upwards and outwards, the supporting leg twisting in the direction of the kick. By this means, the knee comes up and around into the target from the side.

One of the strongest bones in the body is the frontal bone of the skull. A head butt into the attacker's face is very effective, but the chin must be tucked in and the eyes tightly closed on impact. It is possible also to drive the skull backwards into the attacker's face if he is standing close behind. When practising head butt, only gentle movements should be used since banging the head against even a soft pad causes brain damage.

BODY WEAPONS AND TARGETS

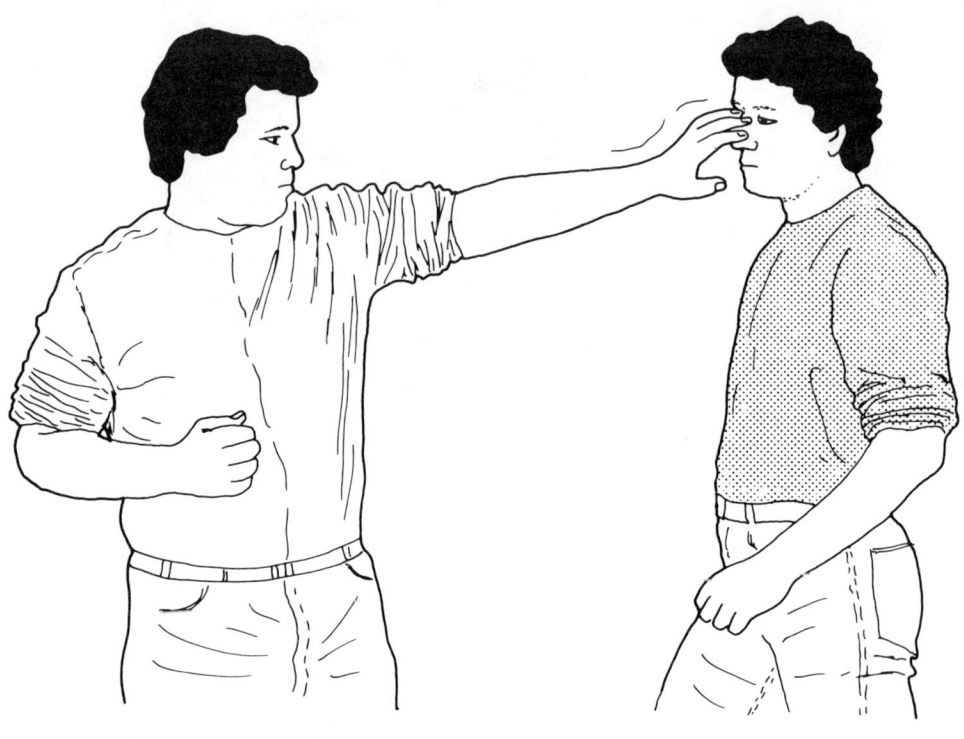

The finger tips

When one is selecting a body weapon to use against a target, the shortest distance must be looked for each time. The closer the weapon is to the target, the more difficult it will be to block. It is illogical, to say the least, to kick someone in the head or butt him in the ankle. Hand techniques should normally be used on targets above the waist, foot techniques to the groin and legs.

The human body has many hidden vulnerable points and some schools of martial art exploit these to stun or even kill an attacker. This takes many years of practice and is beyond the scope of this book. There are, however, a number of more obvious points that can be quickly learned.

The eyes are delicate and protected by strong and involuntary reflexes that pull the head away and close the eyes tightly the moment danger threatens. Any fast move towards the face will cause a reflex blink which can be used to hide a follow-up move. If the fingertips merely graze the covering of the eye,

BODY WEAPONS AND TARGETS

1. *The eyes: these require only the merest graze*

2. *A strike to the side of the jaw can cause head rotation and a KO*

3. *A strike in the throat can be lethal*

4. *Impact here can produce a dramatic backwards jump!*

5. *A blow to the solar plexus winds the attacker*

6. *A strike to the testicles can completely incapacitate*

7. *The knees are a legitimate target for a hard kick*

8. *The insteps are vulnerable to stamping kicks*

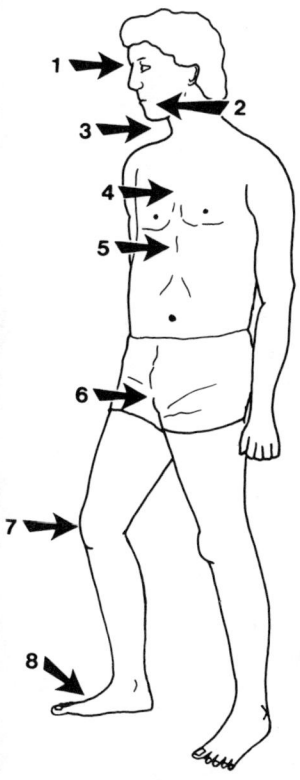

torrents of tears are produced and sight is hopelessly blurred.

The nose is also sensitive; a hard blow on it produces tears and blurring of vision. If the base of the palm is rested on the upper lip and pushed against the nose, the attacker's head will be forced back. A hard blow to the side of the jaw rotates the head violently and causes unconsciousness.

The throat is unprotected by muscle or bone, yet carries major blood vessels and nerves from the brain. Damage to any of these can cause paralysis or unconsciousness. The windpipe can easily be compressed and a blow can rupture its cartilage-reinforced structure, causing death through suffocation.

In the exact centre of the chest, on a level with the nipples, is a point which, if struck sharply, causes the body to fly backwards. This happens because the psoas major muscle is stimulated. Just as a tap on the knee causes the leg to kick out uncontrollably, so an impact on the chest can cause a powerful muscular spasm. This reaction is easy to stimulate in children, where it is known as the Moreau reflex, but in adults it is more difficult to find.

Care must be taken when practising it because a hard blow to the centre of the chest can upset the rhythm of the heart; in extreme cases, death can ensue. The fingertips are placed against the spot on the partner's chest and the touching arm is bent. A sudden sharp muscular contraction slams the heel of the hand into the chest, reinforced by the bent arm suddenly straightening. Provided the blow is sharp enough, the partner will fly backwards.

The solar plexus is where a group of nerves controlling chest muscles and breathing are located close to the surface. A sudden blow there stimulates the nerves, causing the muscles to contract, with consequent interruption in breathing.

The testicles are very sensitive and the lightest impact can cause severe pain. Damage to them causes muscular contraction which interferes with breathing.

The knees are vulnerable targets for the stronger person. A side kick or a thrusting kick can be used to

59

attack them. The insteps are susceptible to a stamping kick, and often a kick to the knee is allowed to continue down the front of the shin, finishing on the insteps.

In conclusion:
Attack the right target with the right weapon.

DEVELOPMENT OF FORCE

Force is the energy used in the execution of strikes, throws, or restraint holds; the type of energy depends upon the application. With strikes, the object is to develop maximum kinetic energy. A billiard ball is quite light when held in the hand, but if it falls from a great height it can cause damage out of all proportion to its resting weight. This is because as it falls, under the influence of gravity, it accelerates to a high speed. When it hits the floor, it gives up its energy as impact.

Physicists have found a relationship between the weight of the moving object and the changing speed at which it is moving. A heavy object can develop a lot of power even when it is moving slowly. A lighter object can develop just as much power, but needs to travel a great deal faster to achieve it. The big man generates great impact with his lumbering swings because there is weight behind them. The smaller person must really wind up and let fly to produce a comparable effect.

A fast-moving small object will bounce off a solid target simply because it is too light to absorb the recoil. Recoil absorbs most of the impact energy and little is transmitted into the target. For this reason, the light person delivering a high energy punch must try to become as heavy as possible. This can be achieved through momentum.

All mass has a resistance to movement, called inertia. Once inertia is overcome, a body will continue until stopped by an outside force. When a speeding car brakes heavily, its passengers will naturally keep moving at the original speed and end up straining against the seat belts. This tendency to keep moving is known as momentum – a powerful

DEVELOPMENT OF FORCE

force. If the full weight of the body is used, a strike will be less likely to bounce off its target.

To throw a powerful punch, the fist must accelerate as quickly as possible. The body must follow behind the blow so that recoil is absorbed and the maximum energy transmitted into the target. Distance from the target is very important: too short and the punch will not be able to accelerate fully; too long and the elbow straightens, bringing acceleration to a sudden stop.

The fist is held loose during the initial phases of the punch and only closes tightly on impact. If it is kept tightly closed from the start, tension in the lower arm muscles inhibits acceleration. The fist must also rotate on impact, going from a palm up position to palm down. This allows it to screw into the target. Rotation must take place precisely on impact; any earlier and the elbow rises, robbing the punch of its energy.

The tightening of the fist on impact is part of an overall muscle spasm called focus. The purpose of focus is to make the body rigid, so maximum power can be transferred into the target. If the body is not rigid, impact energy cannot be efficiently transmitted. The diaphragm also takes part in the spasm, exhaling air in a grunt. The tightening-up of the body also makes it better able to absorb a chance blow.

Developing a high energy punch can be compared to throwing a cricket ball. At the start, the throwing arm trails and weight is on the back foot. The other arm extends well forwards. The hips rotate until they are facing forward but the throwing arm and shoulder lag behind. This causes a tension in the muscles of the back. Tension increases as the thrower begins to transfer weight on to the forward foot. It releases as the throwing arm accelerates up, above and past the shoulder, and is matched by the rapid withdrawal of the leading arm.

A straight punch off the rear hand (called a reverse punch) uses a similar action, except that instead of rising above the shoulder it passes close to the ribs. The leading arm is held palm forwards to mask the following punch. At the moment of impact, weight is still being transferred on to the front leg and the knee

DEVELOPMENT OF FORCE

is well bent. To absorb recoil, the fist must not pass through an imaginary line extending upwards from the shin. A long reverse punch needs a well bent front leg.

The importance of correct stance can be demonstrated with the aid of a partner. The right fist is extended and the elbow locked. The left front knee is bent and the rear leg straightened. The partner now advances on the punch and pushes hard against it. If the punch extends beyond the line of the shin, the front foot will rise from the ground under the partner's applied pressure. This is analogous to the effects of recoil.

If, on the other hand, the front leg is well bent, with the knee over the toes, the foot will not rise under pressure and a punch delivered from this stance will dig into the target. The rear leg need not be rigidly straightened during an actual reverse punch since the moving body absorbs recoil more effectively.

It is possible to snap-punch strongly off the leading fist. The left leg is placed slightly ahead of the right with weight distributed evenly between them. Both hands are at shoulder height, the left slightly leading. As the punch begins, the right hand is first to move, travelling forward, down, and back in a small

The attack is evaded

The defender steps in and uses the elbow. Note the angle of the hips

DEVELOPMENT OF FORCE

A thrust to the jaw uses the same principles

circle. As the right hand is coming back, the left arm is thrown out and the open hand contracts into a fist upon impact. The left hip twists in the direction of the punch and weight is put on the front leg to soak up recoil. Power for the snap punch comes mainly from the pull back of the other fist and the muscle spasm on impact.

It is a good plan to practise using an impact pad made from sheets of closed cell foam. The pad should measure at least a foot square and nine inches thick, so it can be held against the chest. The weight of the body holding the pad gives a realistic sensation of impact and allows the punch's effectivity to be tested. To be effective, the punch has to penetrate into the pad. First contact is made with the punching arm straight; forward body movement gives the required further penetration.

DEVELOPMENT OF FORCE

From cross block the assailant's arm is taken down

Weight is transferred forward

DEVELOPMENT OF FORCE

The hips rotate and an elbow strike . . .

or palm heel thrust is made

DEVELOPMENT OF FORCE

Once the pad can be hit hard (without damage to the hand), it is shifted forwards and backwards, providing a moving target to focus on. Punching against air is of little value except for developing basic co-ordination. Only by striking a pad will deficiencies in technique be shown up.

The problem with any striking technique is that the longer the distance over which it accelerates, the easier it is to block. If the attacker has closed distance, it may not be possible to adopt a correct stance, using the hips for a powerful strike. In this case, a quite powerful punch can be delivered, using muscle spasm alone. The stance is upright and both hands are held well forward, as though to ward off attack. The palms are open and turned towards the attacker. To deliver the punch, the fists suddenly clench, the arms go rigid, and the body rocks forwards on to the front leg. The fist lands with the thumb pointing upwards, rather than the palm down of the snap or reverse punch.

With a little practice, muscle spasm can become so strong that the punch develops a useful impact over distances of not more than five or six inches. Experts can develop as much power with the short range strike as normal people can with the reverse punch.

Simple principles can be applied to make kicks extremely powerful. From a left stance, the right leg is brought up and forwards. The knee bends and the foot points down at the floor. As the knee accelerates up to groin height, the hips are pushed forwards and the lower part of the leg lashes up and out in an arc. To give momentum to the kick, the supporting leg lifts on to the ball of the foot, raising the hips. The back is arched slightly, but the back of the head must be kept directly above the heel of the supporting foot. If it goes beyond that point, the kick becomes unbalanced.

After the instep has connected solidly with the attacker's groin, the lower part of the leg is snapped back again, rather like the crack of a whip. The kick's power comes from the acceleration of the upper part of the leg and the snapping out of the lower. Its rapid snap back makes it difficult to catch.

DEVELOPMENT OF FORCE

A different form of front kick uses the sole of the foot as the impact area. In this case the supporting leg does not straighten and the lower part of the kicking leg is pushed out forcibly like a piston, unlike the passive flicking movement used previously.

For purposes of speed — but not power — a kick may be delivered off the front leg. The front leg is closer to the attacker, so it travels a shorter distance and is less likely to be blocked. Enough weight must first be transferred to the rear leg to allow the front foot to be lifted without loss of balance. The front knee then lifts up sharply and the lower part of the leg lashes out, toes pointing, into the groin.

A turning kick is useful for kicking into the groin when a front kick cannot be used because of the way the attacker is standing. It consists of a sequence of moves culminating in a kick powerful enough to break the attacker's leg. The kick begins from left stance with the upper body turning to the left and leaning away. The right knee rises diagonally and the supporting leg rotates in the same direction as the upper body. As the knee comes to point at the groin, the lower part of the leg lashes out with the toes pointing.

At the moment of impact, the supporting leg has rotated so it is almost facing backwards, and the body is leaning in a straight line away from possible counters. If space is restricted, the turning kick can also be performed off the front leg. Once the basic techniques are acquired, a light punch bag or impact pad can be used to test power.

Developing force in a throw or hold is not so dramatic. There is less need to develop kinetic energy or learn ways to accelerate techniques. The strike provides a distraction during which the throw or hold can be applied. Each consists of a series of movements which depend on leverage for their success. Little effort is used to produce a large response. Focus can improve a throw. The sudden contraction gives extra power and the attacker is more easily toppled over.

Holds depend on smooth application of power, drawing out the attacker's arm, and applying lever-

DEVELOPMENT OF FORCE

The high energy attack needs distance in which to accelerate

age to the joints. The body, rather than arms or shoulders, is used to produce a correct throw. The arms move surprisingly little and leverage is achieved through body movement. Holds too should be used only at the right times, such as when the attacker is off balance or distracted, otherwise a wrestling match develops and the defender's advantage is lost.

Holds work best as receivers of kinetic energy – the attacker pushes, so the defender pulls; the harder the push, the softer the unbalancing pull required.

DEVELOPMENT OF FORCE

The impact is made with the heel and flat of foot

This is the underlying theory of aikido, the martial art 'way of all harmony'. The defender uses distance and evasion to encourage the attacker to over-extend, and then uses this to advantage.

SECTION 3 PRACTICAL (2)
SIMPLE RESPONSES TO ATTACKS

FIRST ECHELON RESPONSES

The first echelon response is a technique designed to distract or to stop an attack when evasion has failed and the attacker is within striking distance or the victim is counter-attacking. In either case, the first echelon response is the initial counter.

In elementary self defence, the first echelon technique is delivered from one of three stances. The first is the aware stance, in which the victim believes there is a possibility of attack and wishes to make ready for it unobtrusively. Typically, the victim steps back a little and turns 45 degrees away from the attacker. This angle ensures that the vulnerable areas are reduced and pulled back from direct attack. The hands are clasped together in front of the groin. From this stance, the victim can move forwards or backwards into a more positive defensive posture.

The second, called ready stance, is used when attack is imminent. The back leg moves a little further back and the hands rise to a guard position. If the left leg is forwards, the left arm will also lead. It is incorrect to stand with, say, the left leg and right hand forward, since this opens up more of the body to attack. The hands are open and the palms are turned slightly towards the attacker, as though trying to placate him. The fingers should be kept together and care taken to ensure they are not grabbed and twisted. Waving closed fists about is not a good idea.

Both arms are held out from the body, with the fingertips about shoulder height and the elbows tucked in. The hands are held close to the midline of the body so there is no gap through which a straight attacking technique can come. It is a good idea to practise ready stance in front of the mirror, since this

FIRST ECHELON RESPONSES

shows up any openings. It should be possible to move about quickly in the stance, changing fluidly from one position to another while making sure that the leading arm and leg coincide. Twisting the hips wipes the front arm across the path of any incoming grasp, deflecting it and allowing the rear hand to counter immediately.

The final position is often called cat stance. Typically, it follows a step back from an attack, with the body weight settling on the back leg, as has previously been described. It is important to keep the body upright and to be balanced in such a way that the front foot can be lifted off the ground without the defender lurching forwards. Cat stance is used when there is insufficient room for a full step back.

Before one uses a first echelon response, care should be taken to ensure it is safe to do so. If the attacker has lunged forwards, evasion must be used, moving the body out of its way while keeping within effective counter-attack range. If the victim has been seized, a first echelon strike will be directly used.

The MAC self defence course is unique in possessing a logical structure, with technique building upon technique. Its syllabus, adapted from the police self defence course, will teach to an elementary level of self defence in a very short time. The individual course teacher may well introduce variations on a particular hold or strike, but the course structure must be maintained if the student is to learn quickly. There are no exceptions to be memorised for recall when the need arises.

The sequences shown are intended to train students in the basic techniques of self defence. At a later stage, practical applications will be shown, but to start with the student must learn how to block effectively and respond quickly in a simplified situation.

In all the training sequences, it is important that the partner makes a strong and accurate attack. If he does not do so, it will not be possible for the defender to learn an effective defence. In the following pages, the attacker is known as 'tori' (pronounced taw-rih), and the victim/defender as 'uke' (pronounced ooh-keh, with the accent on the second

FIRST ECHELON RESPONSES

Evading the attack

syllable). These are common terms used in Japanese martial arts.

In the six basic techniques, uke always begins by standing in an aware stance, with the hands grasped together in front of the groin and the left foot slightly forwards. The hips are turned to the right.

In the first training sequence, tori lunges forwards and tries to grab uke's lapel. Uke evades by stepping back with the right leg and to the side with the left, twisting the hips and fending off the reaching arm.

FIRST ECHELON RESPONSES

Countering with fingers to the eyes

The fending arm is kept well bent and it is important to sidestep no more than the minimum effective distance. No sooner has tori's arm been fended off than uke's blocking arm suddenly flicks out, the fingers grazing across his opponent's eyes. Provided the fingers are moving fast and come close enough, tori will be brought up short and uke will have an opportunity to follow up. Obviously, if the eye strike is completely successful, tori will be incapacitated and uke can escape with no need for further action.

FIRST ECHELON RESPONSES

In the second sequence, the attack and evasion are the same. This time, though, the response is delivered with the reverse hand. The lunge is deflected with the left hand as before and the right hand is used to deliver a claw hand strike to tori's face. It is important that uke twists his hips behind the claw hand, otherwise it will not reach. This hip twist can form the basis for a subsequent strike, as will be seen later. It is also important to keep the fending hand in contact with tori's wrist, so his arm cannot make a second grab if the claw hand is unsuccessful.

Evasion followed by . . .

Claw-hand to the eyes

FIRST ECHELON RESPONSES

Evasion followed by . . .

A groin kick

The third sequence again employs the attack and evasion described for the first, but uke uses a kick as the first echelon response. The attack is fended off and uke kicks off the back leg with a curving action into tori's groin. The kick must snap out and back very quickly, since speed rather than power is important at this stage. The toes point downwards and the instep makes a hard, slapping impact. If this is successful, tori will immediately stop attacking and cover his groin with both hands, allowing uke to escape.

FIRST ECHELON RESPONSES

The fourth, fifth, and sixth sequences all use cross block to a face attack. In the fourth, tori lunges strongly forwards and punches to the face or grabs at the hair. Uke's first move is to step back, taking the vulnerable areas out of range. At the same time, a cross block catches tori's wrist. Uke reaches over with the right hand, seizing tori's wrist and pulling it down to the right side.

It is important that this sequence be practised until it is fluid. The step back, cross block, and pull down must be performed as a single move, so tori has no time to recover composure. During the pull down, it is permissible for uke to twist his hips to the right. This has the effect of drawing out tori's attack and may, if his lunge was strong, cause him to over-balance forwards.

Once tori's arm has been pulled down, uke makes a first echelon strike with his left arm. This lashes out with fingers extended, aiming to strike tori's eyes.

The defender steps back and cross blocks

FIRST ECHELON RESPONSES

The attacker's arm is trapped and brought down

A finger strike to the eyes completes the sequence

FIRST ECHELON RESPONSES

Blocking an attack

In the fifth technique, uke again steps back and cross-blocks, but this time he seizes tori's wrist in his left hand and pulls him down to the left. In this case, right claw hand is used as a first echelon strike.

FIRST ECHELON RESPONSES

The cross block takes the arm the opposite way

A claw hand completes the technique

FIRST ECHELON RESPONSES

A kick to the groin can be effectively used from cross block

In the sixth sequence, tori's arm is not pulled down; uke merely kicks out strongly with the right leg into tori's groin. Once again, the kick is made with the instep of the foot in a fast, snapping movement.

Whatever the attack, the defender always steps back with the right foot. It does not matter whether he uses evasion and fend-off or step back and cross-block; the same three first echelon strikes can be used to good effect in each case.

SECOND ECHELON RESPONSES

There are two kinds of second echelon techniques — strikes and grapples.

Strikes

Second echelon strikes use the dead time generated by a successful first echelon technique to hit a vulnerable point with considerable force. They involve a substantial commitment from which it is difficult to withdraw. A second echelon kick, for example, deliberately throws uke's body off balance; equilibrium is restored by impact with tori's body. Typically, these responses involve a long movement during which the technique is accelerated by a combination of hip twist and shoulder movement. When used alone they can sometimes be blocked by an aware tori, so they are best deployed after a lower impact first echelon strike.

It should not be taken as an absolute rule that second echelon techniques must follow first echelon counters. Athletic and co-ordinated people can use them readily at any stage and there may always be the chance to use one unexpectedly — if tori slips and falls as he attacks, for instance.

Several different high energy strikes can be used in the second echelon. In keeping with the training pattern already established, six are shown as basic techniques for practice purposes. To avoid complication, they are not accompanied by the preceding first echelon strike. The practical applications are dealt with elsewhere in the book.

Like the first echelon series, all techniques start with uke in a left aware stance. In the first example, tori steps forwards to grasp at uke's lapel or to punch to the chest. Uke steps diagonally back with the right leg and fends off the arm. The diagonal step is quite short, since it is important to remain within range. A short step directly backwards could mean the attack still managed to reach. The fend-off uses rather more hip twist than previously and the right arm is withdrawn, elbow outwards, to the side of the body. The hips suddenly twist back to face tori and, after a short time lag, the shoulders are released. The right arm flies forward as an elbow strike to the side of tori's jaw.

To maximise impact, the fending arm is withdrawn at the same speed as that of the elbow strike going out, and body weight is transferred on to the front leg. Since elbow strike is a short range technique, it requires a considerable move forwards on the left leg to close to effective range. The right drags behind on the ball of the foot, preventing the stance from stretching out and becoming ungainly. To maximise range, the back arches and the face is pulled back out of danger.

The second technique uses the same attack and fend-off, but right palm heel is used instead of elbow strike. Because palm heel is a medium range high energy technique, uke does not have to close range to the same extent as in the former example. However, the range must be right if the strike is to develop its full power. Too long a range over-extends it; too short a range means it does not have sufficient distance in which to reach maximum speed. Ideally, the elbow will just be straightening as contact is made with tori's jaw. People who can punch competently may choose reverse punch in place of palm heel.

The third technique also uses a diagonal step back and fend-off, but uke does not have to close with tori. His upper body leans to the left, twisting away from tori's outstretched arm. The hips follow the shoulders, and uke swivels on the ball of his left foot. The right foot lifts off the ground with knee bent, travelling up and around into tori's stomach. A strong person can develop enough force with this turning kick to cause serious internal injuries.

The fourth technique is in response to a punch to the face or a grab for the hair. Uke makes safe by quickly stepping directly back a short distance with the right foot and cross-blocking. He catches tori's wrist with his left hand and pulls him down to the left. At the same time, uke's right arm pulls back and bends, elbow out, palm of hand towards tori's face. Uke steps quickly forward on the left leg, twisting his hips to the left. The right leg drags up behind and uke strikes tori in the side of the jaw with elbow strike.

The fifth technique uses the same attack and response – seizing tori's wrist with the left hand and pulling it down. At the same time, uke's right elbow pulls back. The striking hand is held palm forwards and fingers rotated to the right. On impact, the palm heel rotates so the fingers turn vertically upwards, and the strike catches tori full in the nose. A normal reverse punch may be substituted for palm heel, but should be aimed at the nose, not the mouth, as teeth are surprisingly unhygienic and can cause serious septic wounds if they break the skin.

In the sixth technique uke again cross blocks and takes tori's arm to the left. This time, the hips rise up and forwards, causing the back to arch. The right knee lifts off and the foot points at the floor as it is accelerated up and snapped out into the groin. The knee must accelerate as quickly as possible and reach correct height when it is pointing at tori's groin. The back must be well arched as the instep makes contact, so full body weight is put into the kick. The right arm is not used and the elbow is kept at the side of the body.

In conclusion:
>Use high energy strikes to vulnerable points to injure the attacker, but only when their use is unavoidable.

Grapples

The second echelon technique need not be a strike; it can be a restraint hold or a throw. Grappling techniques are more selective than strikes but they are difficult to apply as they involve complicated moves and require strength and agility. A number of extremely difficult grappling techniques which are highly effective look deceptively simple. Some of them would be included in a longer course, but in this MAC course only the simplest grapples with the widest application have been selected.

Grapple techniques are used after a distraction; only highly competent people can apply them without. As with second echelon strikes, there are rare

SECOND ECHELON RESPONSES

From evasion, seize wrist

Step forward and rotate the arm

exceptions to this rule. The grapple is applied on the move and tori is never allowed to regain the initiative. If anything goes wrong, it is better to release and look for a second opportunity.

There are six grapples, which are first practised in training. The first technique is wrist trap. Tori steps

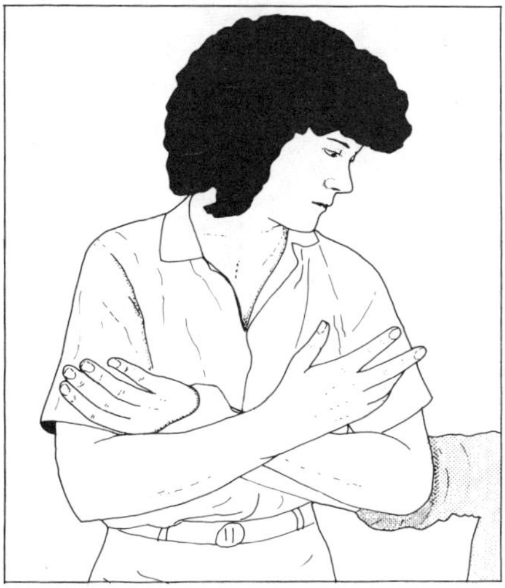

SECOND ECHELON RESPONSES

Lock arm over, continue drawing out

Detail of hold

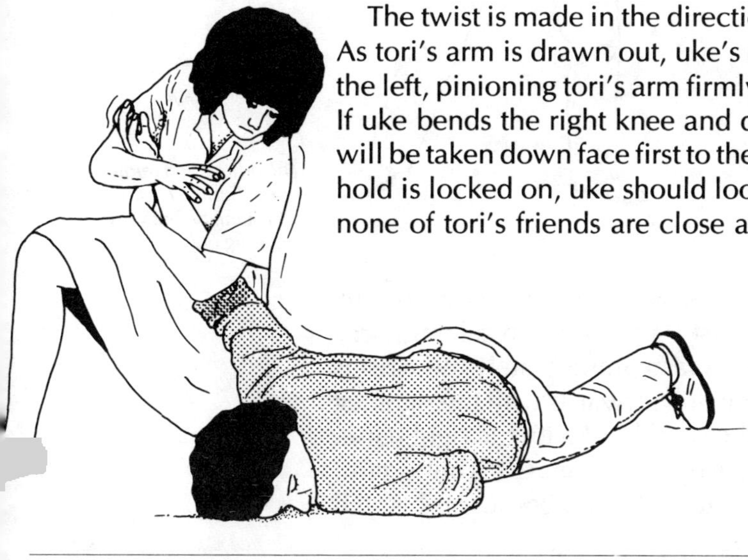

Attacker is taken to floor

forward and attempts to push uke in the chest or to grab his lapel. Uke steps diagonally back a short distance from aware stance and fends the arm off. He uses his left fending arm to keep contact with tori's wrist, which uke seizes in an overhand grasp. Without hesitating, uke now steps out to the right with the right leg, drawing out and twisting tori's arm.

The twist is made in the direction of uke's fingers. As tori's arm is drawn out, uke's right wrist overlies the left, pinioning tori's arm firmly against the chest. If uke bends the right knee and drops the hips, tori will be taken down face first to the ground. Once the hold is locked on, uke should look up to check that none of tori's friends are close at hand.

SECOND ECHELON RESPONSES

From evasion, the wrist is seized

The other hand reinforces the hold, thumb crossing thumb whilst the defender is stepping out

The second grapple, wrist turn, starts in exactly the same way as wrist trap, with uke seizing tori's wrist in an overhand grasp. Immediately the wrist is seized, uke steps out and forwards with the right leg while reinforcing the wrist hold with the right hand. The way in which the right hand grasps is important: uke's right thumb actually crosses over his left

SECOND ECHELON RESPONSES

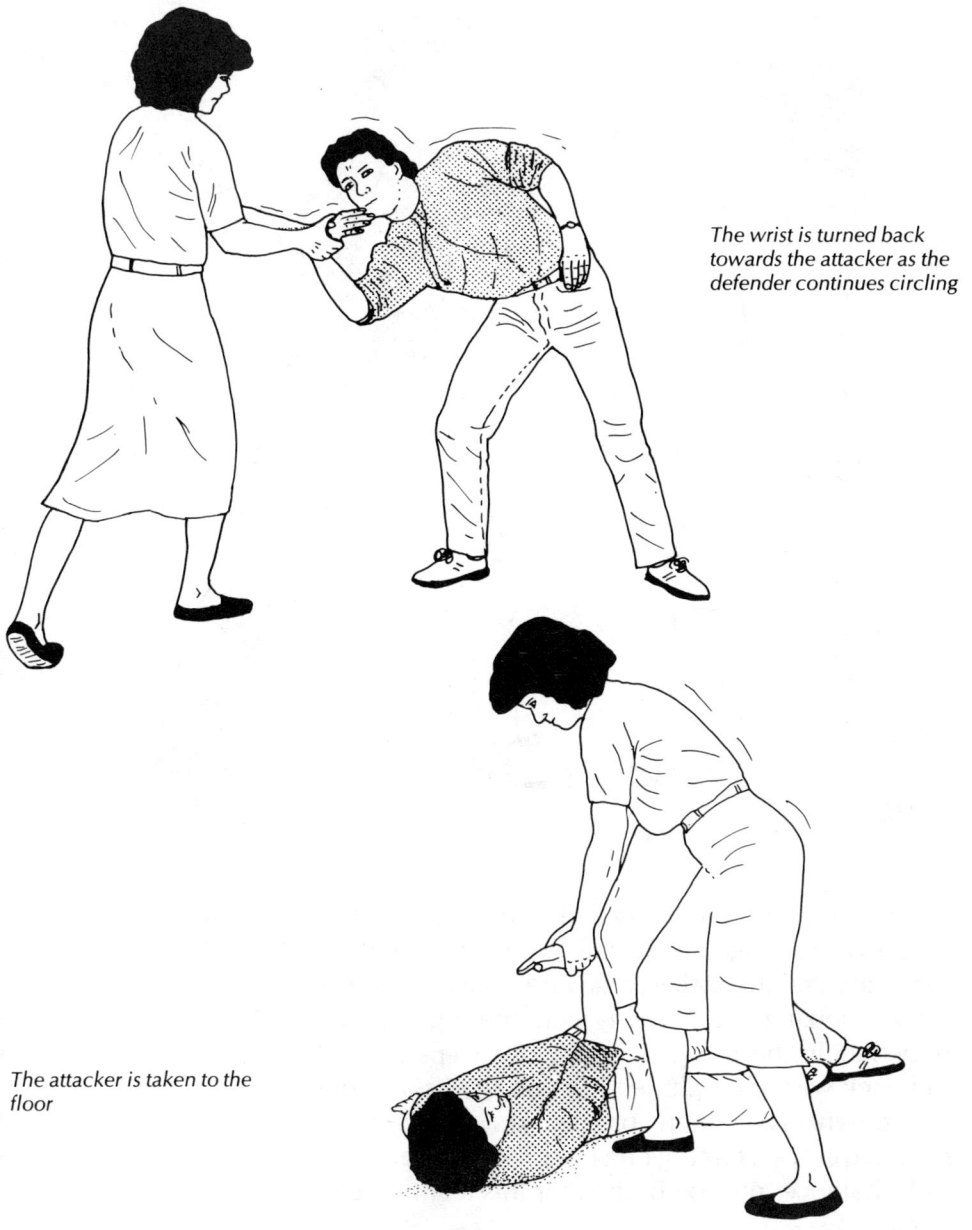

The wrist is turned back towards the attacker as the defender continues circling

The attacker is taken to the floor

thumb at the back of tori's hand. Uke steps behind his own right leg and suddenly swivels his hips, at the same time pushing on the thumbs and forcing tori's wrist to bend. Provided the left foot continues swinging around behind the right, the wrist turn will drop tori on to his back. It is important that the wrist is bent in its normal direction and tori's elbow kept flexed.

SECOND ECHELON RESPONSES

From cross block the arm is taken down

The third grapple is called push down. Tori attacks with a lunge for the hair or punch to the face. Uke steps straight back from aware stance and cross blocks, seizing tori's wrist with the right hand. Immediately the grasp is made, uke steps around and back with the right leg, drawing tori's arm out and down. Uke then presses down on tori's extended elbow, forcing him face first to the ground. Tori's balance must be broken for this technique to work.

When uke is pushing down, his left knee should be nearly into the elbow. Full body weight can then be brought to bear. If tori tries to resist, a hammerfist strike can be used. This is particularly painful against the extended elbow, and if sufficient force is used, tori will quickly co-operate. It is possible to hold tori flat on the floor by kneeling on the back of the elbow.

SECOND ECHELON RESPONSES

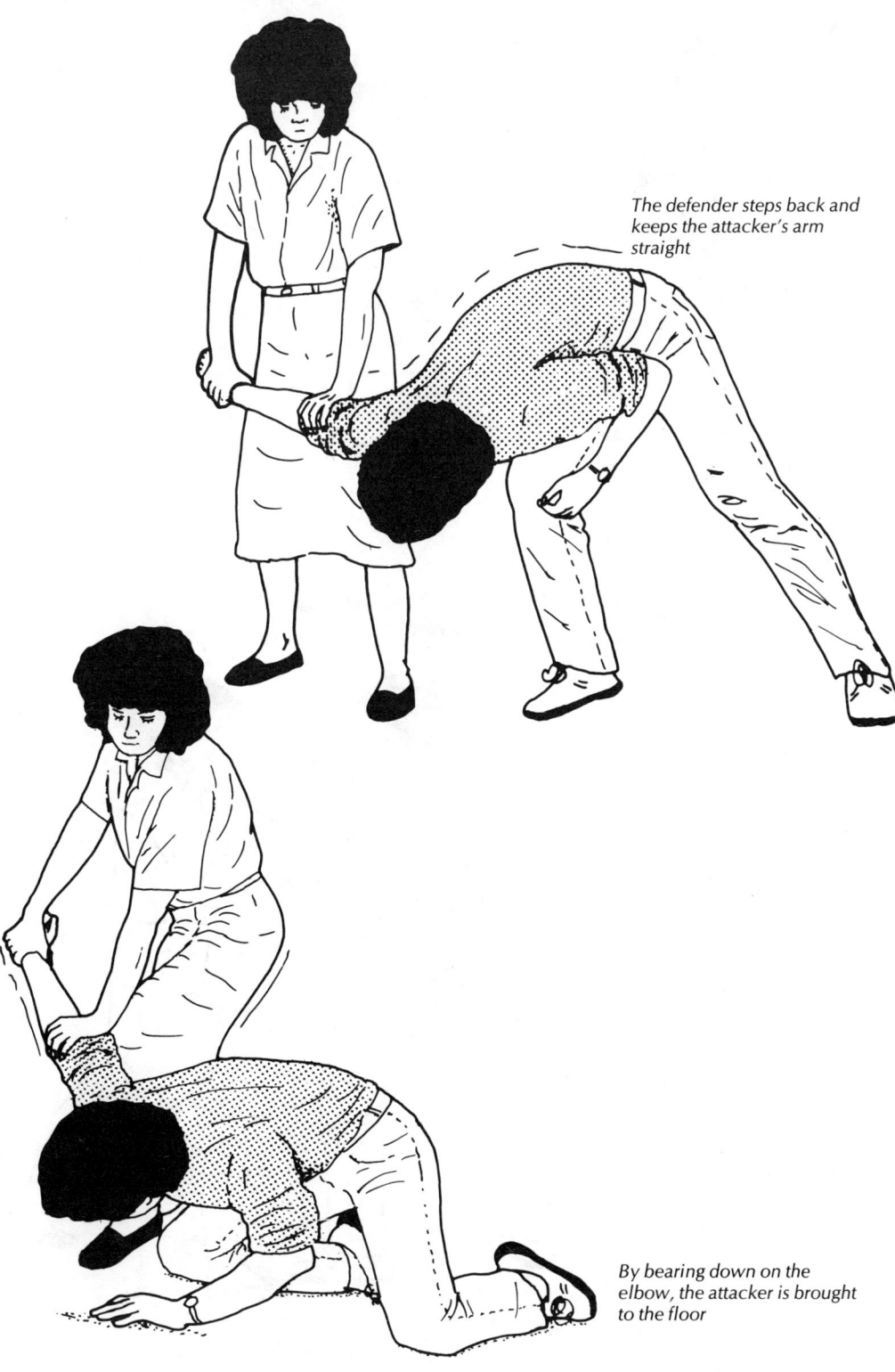

The defender steps back and keeps the attacker's arm straight

By bearing down on the elbow, the attacker is brought to the floor

SECOND ECHELON RESPONSES

From cross block, the arm is taken down

The defender steps in

SECOND ECHELON RESPONSES

The fourth technique is known as backwards trip. Once again, tori attacks to the face or head and is cross-blocked. His wrist is seized with the left hand and pulled down while uke steps diagonally forward with the right. His advancing right leg skims to the outside of tori's and then powerfully hooks back, catching him behind his knee. At this point, uke has actually crashed into tori, pushing him back onto his trapped right leg. Uke's right bicep catches tori across the throat, forcing his head back so he loses his balance and topples over his rear leg.

The trip is made easier if uke hooks back on the trapped leg at the same time as tori is body-charged. It is also important that tori's head is forced back, otherwise it will be difficult to break his balance and he may counter with a backwards trip of his own.

The attacker is caught across the throat with the biceps whilst the defender steps through and insinuates her leg behind his

Using sudden body weight, the attacker is unbalanced

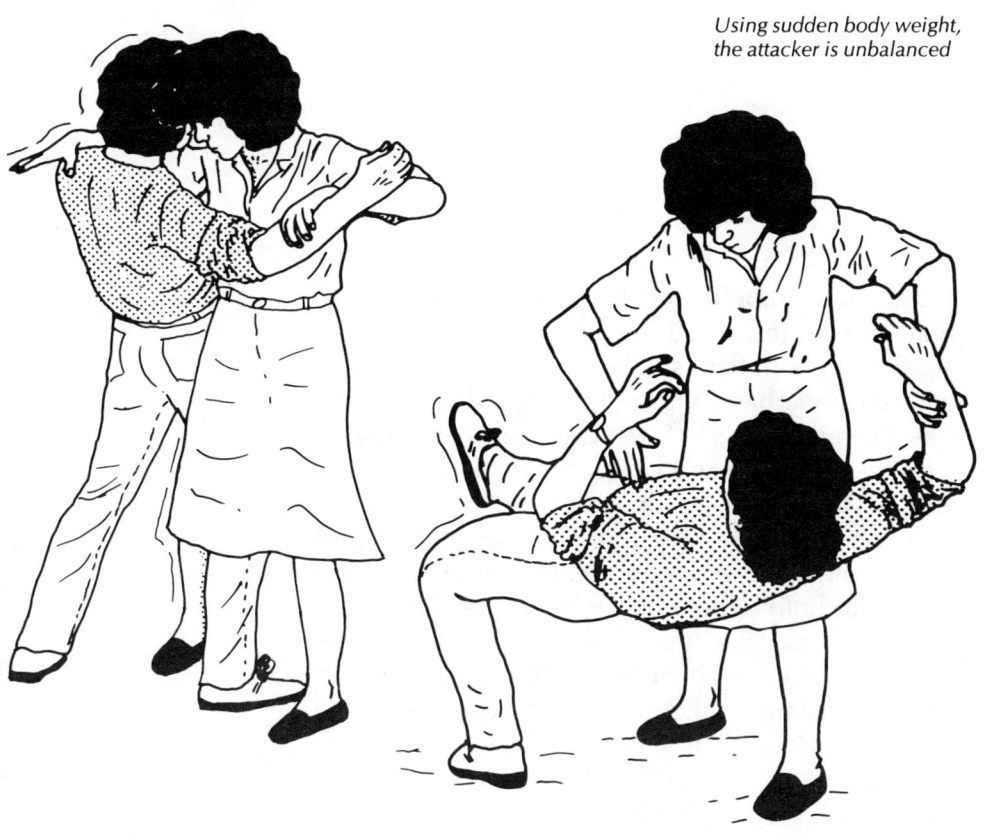

SECOND ECHELON RESPONSES

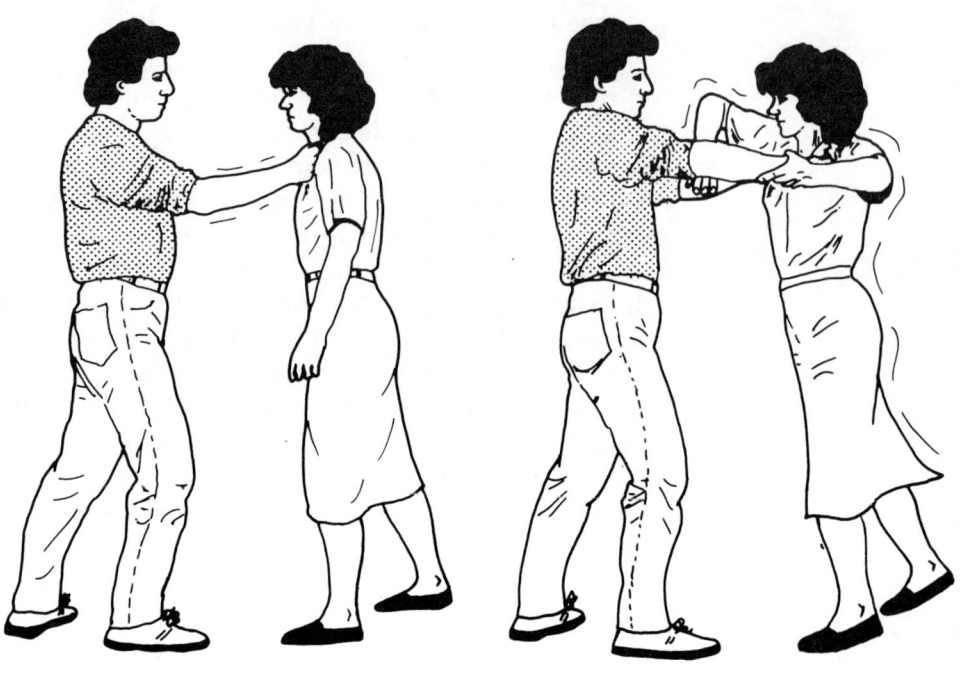

Attacker grabs lapel

His grasping wrist is held and defender's arm loops over

The fifth grapple is called shoulder throw. To practise this, tori should be allowed to grasp uke's lapels with both hands. Uke seizes tori's right wrist with an underhand grasp and loops the right arm over the top of tori's left arm. Uke then steps forward with his right foot and brings his right arm up and around the back of tori's upper arm, near the shoulder. Uke's right leg continues stepping on past tori's right. He then gives a sudden hip twist that ends with both opponents facing the same way. As the hip turns, uke lifts with the right arm while dragging around with the left and bending forwards. Tori is unbalanced and taken over uke's thigh on to his back. This technique, like backwards trip, depends on a smooth flow of movement, with uke getting below tori's centre of gravity.

SECOND ECHELON RESPONSES

Stepping in, the arm loops up behind his shoulder

The body twists suddenly

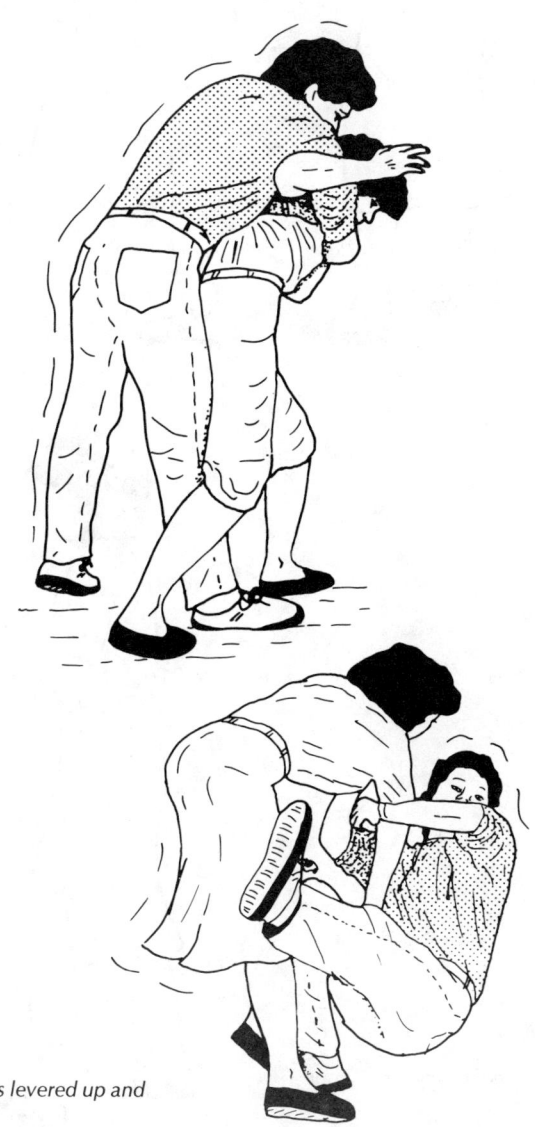

The attacker is levered up and over

SECOND ECHELON RESPONSES

The defender's arm is seized

The seizing arm is trapped

SECOND ECHELON RESPONSES

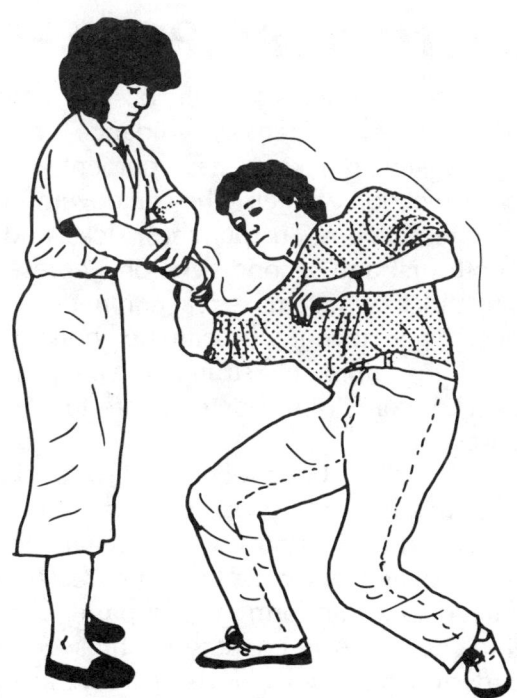

The defender steps around. The trapped arm is rotated, bringing attacker to his knees.

The sixth and final basic grapple technique is wrist circle. It looks easy in comparison with other wrist holds, but is actually very difficult to apply properly. It is practised in the form of an escape move, with tori having grasped uke's right wrist with his own right hand. Uke traps the grasping arm by placing the left arm palm down on the back of tori's wrist. Stepping forward with the rear leg, uke bends tori's captured arm at the elbow and then rotates his wrist in a circle. The direction of the circle is in line with the overlying fingers of uke's left hand.

Provided tori's elbow is kept bent, the rotation of his wrist will make him drop to his knees and remain there. While uke is applying the wrist circle he should hold his elbows close to his body and keep the captured wrist on the centre line. Once tori is subdued, uke is able to look around and make sure there are no other imminent problems.

In conclusion:
Use a grapple to immobilise or throw the attacker.

PRACTICAL RESPONSES

Once the student understands the basic principles of self defence — awareness/avoidance, distance, timing, evasion/blocking, development of force, and body weapons/targets — he can develop skill in the basic techniques. The punches, kicks, and grapples, both first and second echelon, represent the building blocks which make real competence in self defence. Basic techniques can be thought of as letters of the alphabet, strung together to make words. The words of self defence are the practical responses.

They use several basic techniques, one following the other in a logical progression. For instance, uke may respond to tori's attack with a left handed finger flick to the eyes. In the dead time this creates, a right palm heel strike can form the first part of a second echelon counter. As it impacts, the hips are twisted forwards and the rear heel is rising from the ground. This is the perfect lead-in to a powerful turning kick that catches tori as he falls back from the palm heel.

Since each basic technique is fairly complicated in itself, the student cannot be expected to link them together unless each can be performed competently and without conscious thought. In this section, the attacks are more forceful and realistic, with tori actually trying to strike or grab uke. As competence increases, so does speed of attack until, at the end of the course, uke can respond automatically to a sudden and unspecified attack, after which tori does not wait for a counter-attack. If uke has not mastered timing, he should return to basic practice until this has been achieved.

Realism is the key to the practical responses. The striking counter-attacks will be pulled short of causing actual damage (uke will have checked that they generate sufficient force by trying them against the impact pad) and tori must simulate the imagined effects. This means that if the first echelon strike is to the eyes, tori must act as though his eyes had been touched; both hands will fly to his face and the attack will cease. Similarly, if there is a kick into the groin, tori must simulate a reaction by dropping both hands there.

Obviously this kind of practice can be fun, and students will learn quickly if they are interested. One should never forget the purpose behind the course, though, and a high standard must be set for each technique. Sloppiness must be avoided if accidents are not to happen. During the practical responses, techniques are used quickly in a simulation of reality. Lack of concentration will lead to injury to one or both partners.

While tori must avoid unreasonable compliance with the counters used, he must not deliberately make things more difficult for uke. When both parties know exactly what is about to happen, tori's responses will not be fully lifelike. Some aim their techniques not where uke is, but where they know he is going to be. This is not helpful and must be avoided. On each attack, tori must be free of any preconceptions except the validity of the attack.

By the time both partners come to train on practical responses, they should be able to apply grapple techniques effectively, within the limits imposed by their relative sizes. The small uke can get away with nothing in a grapple against a larger tori. This means that smaller people must reach a high standard to maximise their chances.

Every opportunity must be taken to practise with different people. It is all too easy to become used to one's training partner's speed, reach and timing; this is not a good thing. It is good practice for tori to vary the attacks used during these sequences. Appropriate responses will work regardless of the particular attack used, as long as the principles of evasion and timing are observed. Uke must be aware of the opportunities to counter-attack and take them as they come.

In keeping with the structure of the course, six practical responses are described. The first involves the now familiar evasion and fend-off. Tori will have to step forward to attack because uke has used distance correctly and has stepped back into left aware stance. Uke watches tori's face, looking for the telltale narrowing of the eyes that warns of an immi-

PRACTICAL RESPONSES

The attack is evaded

A first echelon strike is made to the eyes

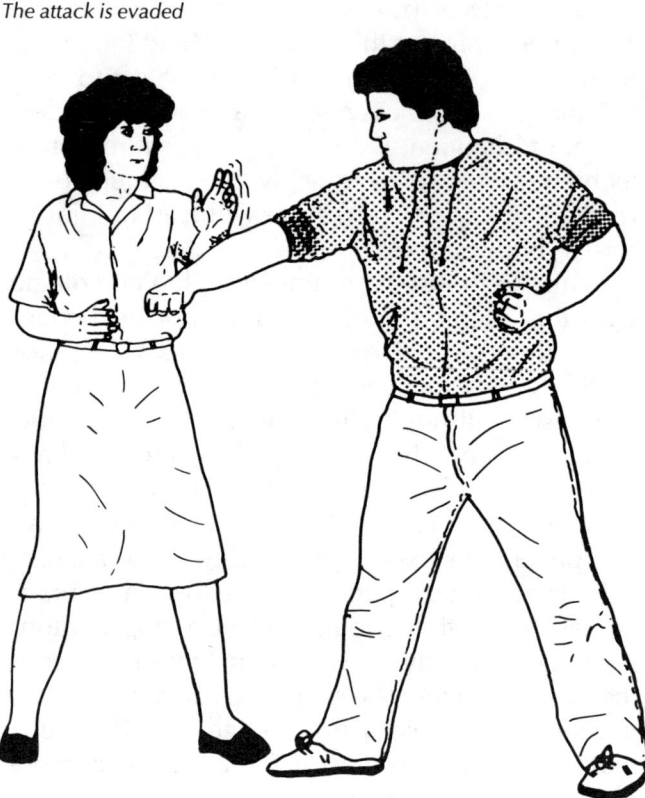

nent, committed attack. When he sees this, uke immediately makes safe by moving diagonally back a short distance into ready stance. If the timing is right, tori and uke move virtually simultaneously.

Tori jabs with the leading fist to uke's chest; uke, now out of distance and to one side, fends off the arm. It is important that tori's jab is withdrawn quickly, and this means that uke's fend probably will not even make contact with it. Nevertheless, the fend is performed as a light, fast move. If it does manage to contact tori's jab and slap it off course, that is a bonus.

There is no hesitation in uke's movements as he completes the fend-off. The fending arm travels in a small circle, quickly reversing direction and lashing out at tori's eyes. There must be little delay between

PRACTICAL RESPONSES

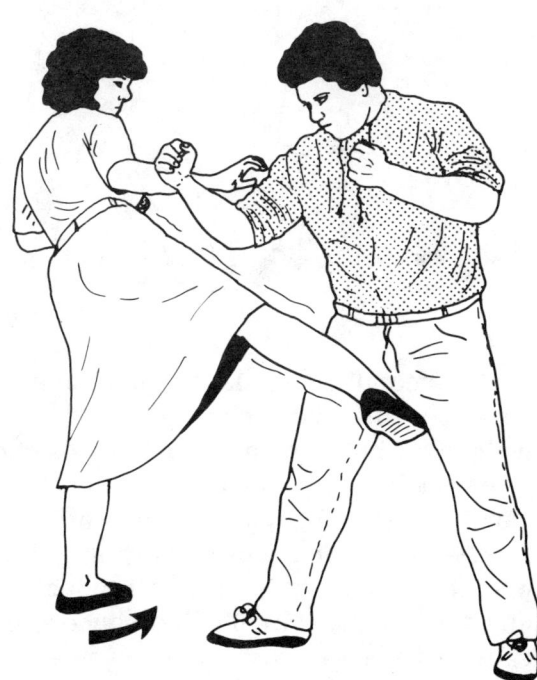

A powerful groin kick concludes the sequence

the fend-off and the first counter-attack, since a jab can form part of a volley of blows. It is important to interrupt the attacker's movement at the earliest possible moment.

Once the eye strike makes contact, tori will immediately clasp both hands over his face and possibly turn away. As he does so, uke quickly swivels on the front (left) leg and delivers a powerful kick into tori's groin. This second echelon strike will drop tori to his knees, allowing uke to escape.

The different targeting described above increases the chance of a successful second echelon strike because the first strike takes tori's hands up to his face, leaving the groin undefended. Wherever possible, strikes should be alternately targeted high and low.

The attack is evaded

The second technique uses the same attack and response. This time, the fending hand is not quickly withdrawn but remains near tori's extended arm. Uke twists the right hip forwards and attacks with a claw hand to tori's face. As with all first echelon strikes, the movement uses little power, but speed is important. If the claw hand is fast enough and travelling direct to the eyes, it will produce a reflex blink causing the head to turn away. Reverse claw hand is quite a long strike and the chances of it actually hitting the face are small because tori probably has time to withdraw his head.

Although tori is unlikely to bring both hands to his eyes, he may do so. While uke's claw hand is nearing its target, his fending left hand should be reaching for tori's wrist and grasping it in an overarm grip. With no hesitation, uke steps around and applies wrist turn. If the claw hand is partly successful, tori will pull against uke's grip, bending the elbow and making it easier for him to apply the wrist turn.

Claw hand has to be used without hesitation because tori has another fist ready. However, uke's diagonal position means that to use that fist, tori would have to twist his body and reach out. This attack would be unstable and unlikely to succeed, and would present uke with a second opportunity for a counter, should the first one fail.

PRACTICAL RESPONSES

First echelon response is a claw hand to the face

The extended wrist is seized

A wrist twist is applied

PRACTICAL RESPONSES

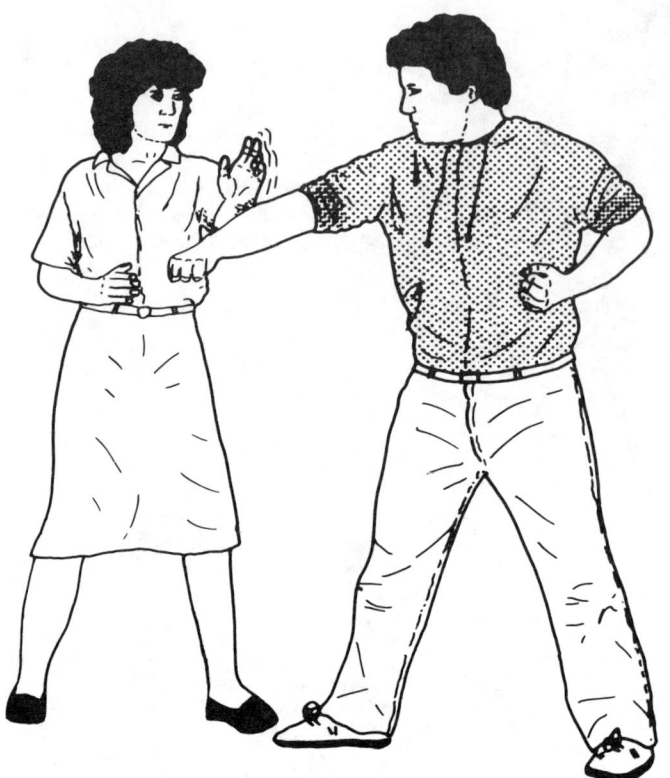

The attack is evaded

The third technique also uses a straight punch/fend-off. Uke's fending left arm remains near tori's punch and an attempt is made to grab it before it is withdrawn. The timing of the move is such that as uke is fending, he is simultaneously kicking from the right leg into tori's groin. The kick used is a fast, snapping movement involving great speed but little power. Even if it does not make contact, it will still bring tori's head down and distract him from using a follow-up attack.

If the kick does catch tori's groin, he will pull back both arms; uke must be prepared to counter this with a strong pull. After kicking, uke lands wide and jerks on tori's arm to pull him forward and off balance. Because tori is already leaning in response to the groin kick, this should not be too difficult. The strong pull forwards is followed by a wrist trap. The key for success in this technique is the rapid kick immediately following the step back.

PRACTICAL RESPONSES

Whilst maintaining contact with the attacking arm, a first echelon strike distracts

A wrist trap is applied

The fourth technique uses a cross block allied to a step back. This is always a good make-safe and, when uke is in doubt, it should be done by default. Uke starts in left aware stance and tori makes a sudden, strong lunge for the face or hair. Uke steps back a short distance with the rear leg and cross-blocks. If space is short, uke can transfer his weight back and take up left cat stance.

As soon as the cross block catches the attacker's wrist, uke's right hand seizes and pulls it down. If the block is properly timed, it will make use of the attack's forward motion to pull tori on to the first echelon strike. As tori's arm is being pulled down, uke uses a left hand finger strike to the eyes. If successful, it will make tori pull both hands back to his face, leaving the groin open for a powerful second echelon kick. If the eye strike is less successful, tori will still turn his head away and not see the following kick.

In real life, it is difficult to make a cross block work like this against a fast jab off the front hand. If the jab is committed – that is, tori intends to hit and injure with it – he will bring weight forwards and uke's step back may cause him to over-extend. In this position, tori is still vulnerable to the first echelon strike. If he jabs without commitment, uke's use of correct distancing makes it miss its target.

The attack is blocked

PRACTICAL RESPONSES

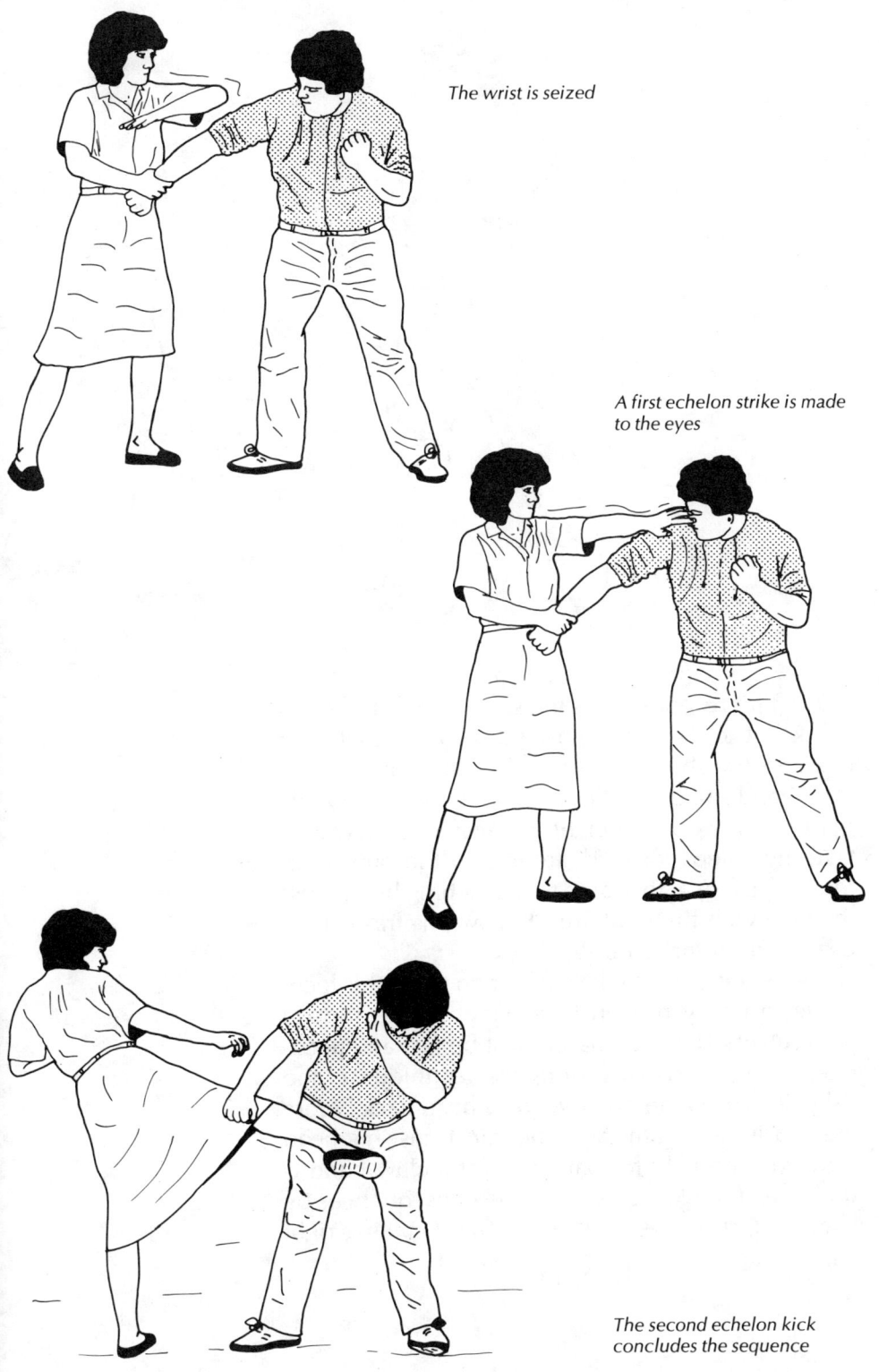

The wrist is seized

A first echelon strike is made to the eyes

The second echelon kick concludes the sequence

PRACTICAL RESPONSES

Cross block is made

The fifth response uses the same attack and cross block but tori's arm is now taken by uke's left. If possible, tori should be pulled forwards on to a right claw hand strike to the eyes. During its delivery, his right leg lifts up as weight is transferred forwards. Uke then steps forward strongly to the outside of tori's right leg, at the same time catching him across the face with the right arm. Backwards trip is then used to drop tori on to his back.

Lighter ukes must take care when using this technique lest they run on to a punch or be tripped themselves. The claw hand must be fast and accurate; without this diversion, the technique is too risky. It is important to drive tori's head back before the trip is used, otherwise he can thrust his head forwards and fight for balance. If the claw hand is unsuccessful, uke can escape the consequences by kneeing tori in the groin with the advancing right leg.

PRACTICAL RESPONSES

A first echelon strike is made to the eyes

The defender steps through and applies a backwards trip

The attacker is toppled backwards

PRACTICAL RESPONSES

The final response has tori's arm caught in the cross block and uses a fast groin kick to collapse him forwards. As before, the kick starts immediately uke's right leg has touched down from the step back, flicking out quickly but without great force. Tori's arm is jerked out to the side as uke lands and immediately steps back, applying a left hammerfist to the extended elbow in a push down.

The kick to the groin must be light enough to bring the head forwards, yet not hard enough to floor tori. For the sequence to work, uke must maintain contact with tori's attacking arm. If it is pulled away, no attempt should be made to seize it. The programmed sequence halts at that point and uke switches to a descending elbow strike to the back of tori's head. If the kick is sufficiently hard, uke can make a safe escape without the need for any follow-up.

The final stage of the push down should not be used if any of the attacker's accomplices are nearby.

Once students have become competent in developing a free-flowing sequence of moves against the standard attacks described above, they should try them against different attacks. At first, uke will know what the attack is to be, and he must select the correct response to it. If tori attacks with a kick, uke will step diagonally back for a fend-off; he will not attempt a cross-block to a non-existent high strike. Certainly the step back/cross block combination will make safe, but it will not provide so effective a platform for the counter-attack.

With further practice, uke will learn to identify tori's attack at an early stage and make not only the safest response but also the most appropriate. The result of this vital training is to improve uke's ability to deal with any unprogrammed attack, using the techniques taught on the course.

In conclusion:
   Use timing to move at the right time.
   Evade tori's attack.
   Counter with a first echelon strike immediately.
   Allow for tori's response to the first echelon strike.
   Complete the sequence with a second echelon technique.

PRACTICAL RESPONSES

Cross block is applied

First echelon strike is made to the groin

Arm is taken and a push down applied

The extended elbow is knelt on

SECTION 4 PRACTICAL (3) PUTTING TECHNIQUES AND RESPONSES INTO PRACTICE

ESCAPES

Escapes form an interesting part of the self defence syllabus. They are the techniques to use when the attacker has managed to grab hold of the victim. The purpose of the grab will be to restrict the victim's movements, preventing escape and reducing the possibilities of evasion. A lapel grab will hold the victim so that a punch or butt can be used; a headlock will allow the attacker to drag the victim into a car. Strangles are attacks in their own right, causing the victim to lose consciousness rapidly. The chosen escape technique must quickly and effectively free the victim, allowing him to return to a position where the normal rules of self defence can apply.

Escaping from a grab or hold is more a matter of logic than physical skill. The victim simply considers which body weapons are available and what targets they can be applied to. Powerful striking techniques must be ruled out where there is no distance in which to accelerate them and no stable stance to provide a solid platform for delivery. Counter-holds often cannot be directly used because the victim cannot generate the body movement necessary to execute them. Instead, sole reliance must be placed on low energy strikes as the first line of response. Since these have a low impact force, the susceptible targets are narrowed to the eyes and the groin.

The nature of escape moves makes them difficult to practise. In the self defence class, it is not acceptable for uke to grasp tori's groin. A simulation is necessary, and it is possible only to determine whether the escape technique selected in a particular situation can reach its target.

ESCAPES

Escape from side head lock

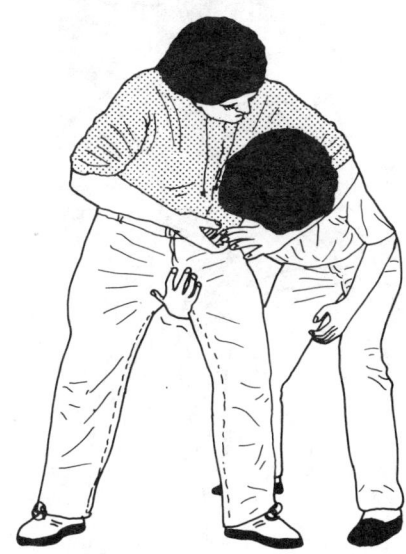

The attacker's groin is seized

In the first escape technique, tori has caught uke in a head chancery, or side headlock. This is uncomfortable but not immediately dangerous. From it, though, the attacker can ram the victim's head into a wall, or attack the face. If uke simply tries to pull free, his face can become lacerated. If tori is tripped or thrown, he may keep hold of uke's head and use it to prevent him from falling. Attempts to unbalance tori can therefore result in damage to the neck, so should be avoided.

The aim must be to get tori to release his grip, so uke can pull free and either escape or use a second echelon technique. An evaluation of the situation shows that uke has both arms and both legs free. Tori's groin is open to attack because he is using both arms for the headlock. Uke therefore reaches quickly between tori's legs and smacks upwards into the groin. Tight trousers sometimes make it difficult to grasp anything, but a firm blow with the palm of the hand will make tori release his hold suddenly.

ESCAPES

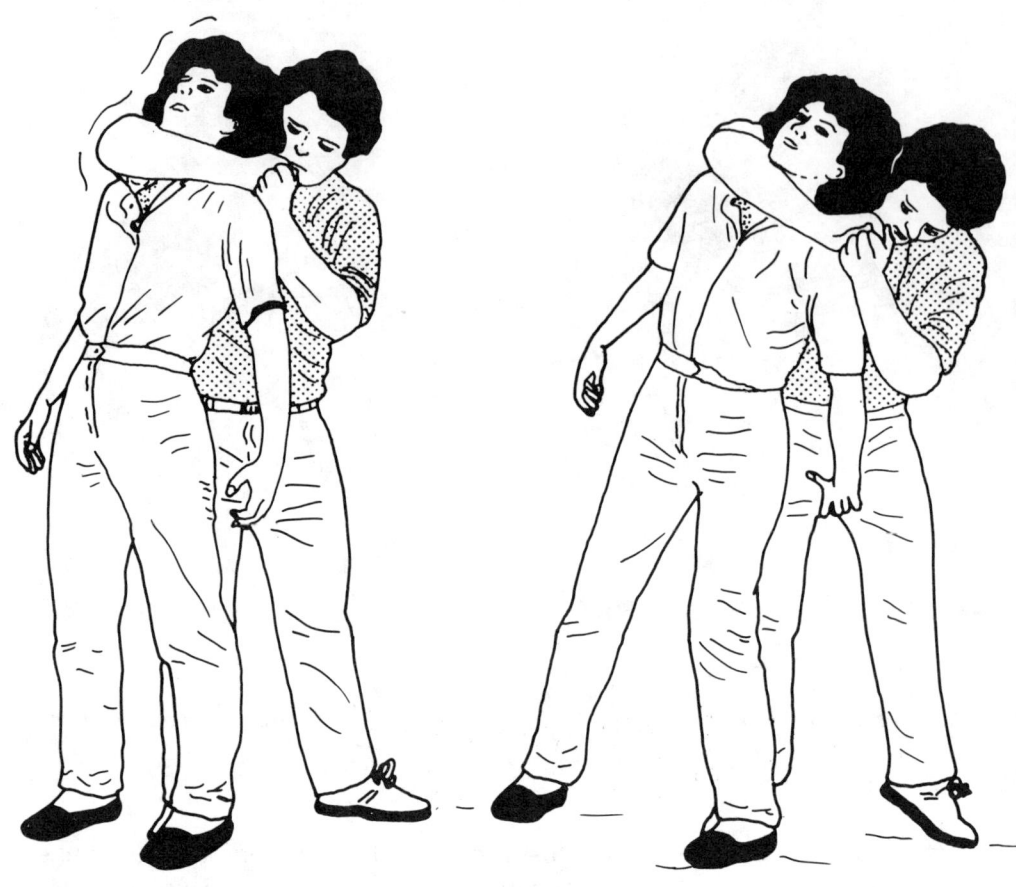

Rear strangle is applied to the victim

The attacker's groin is seized

The second technique involves a rear strangle, where tori has approached from behind and brought an arm across uke's windpipe. Speed is important when dealing with this technique because unconsciousness can quickly result. Uke's arms and legs are free but he cannot use them to develop a good impact.

Many self defence courses advise using a back elbow to loosen the throat grip, but this is impractical and ineffective, first because it requires uke to locate tori's solar plexus accurately. Second, uke's elbow must be accelerated to the point where it is capable of winding tori; this requires body movement and a degree of hip twist, neither of which are available. It is also pointless to try to stamp on tori's feet. They cannot be seen from uke's position, and

ESCAPES

The defender drops her stance...

and shoulder throws the attacker

whether they are actually stamped on or not is a matter of luck. If uke does connect, then all tori need do is pull him back off balance.

Uke's only sensible response in a rear strangle is to reach back and feel for tori's groin. If this is struck, repeatedly if necessary, with a hammerfist, tori will relax the hold. Once the grip loosens, uke can reach up and grasp tori's arm close to the elbow with the right hand and at the wrist with the left. Uke then steps back and around with the right foot and bends both knees to get below tori's centre of gravity. A sudden twisting pull levers tori diagonally forward and over the extended leg. Stronger and more agile ukes can shoulder-throw directly if they get under tori's centre of gravity.

If an attacker succeeds in taking hold of the lapel with a single hand, a quick response is called for. Stance is important; uke should stand at an angle to tori, not directly facing him. As tori grabs hold, uke must seize his wrist in an overarm hold and claw hand strike to the eyes as quickly as possible. This will cause tori's grasp to loosen. Uke then steps back and twists around, applying a wrist trap. There should be no delay in using the claw hand, otherwise tori will throw a punch which, because of the grasp, uke will be unable to evade. As the lapel grasp is made, so the claw hand is used.

The victim is seized in a lapel hold

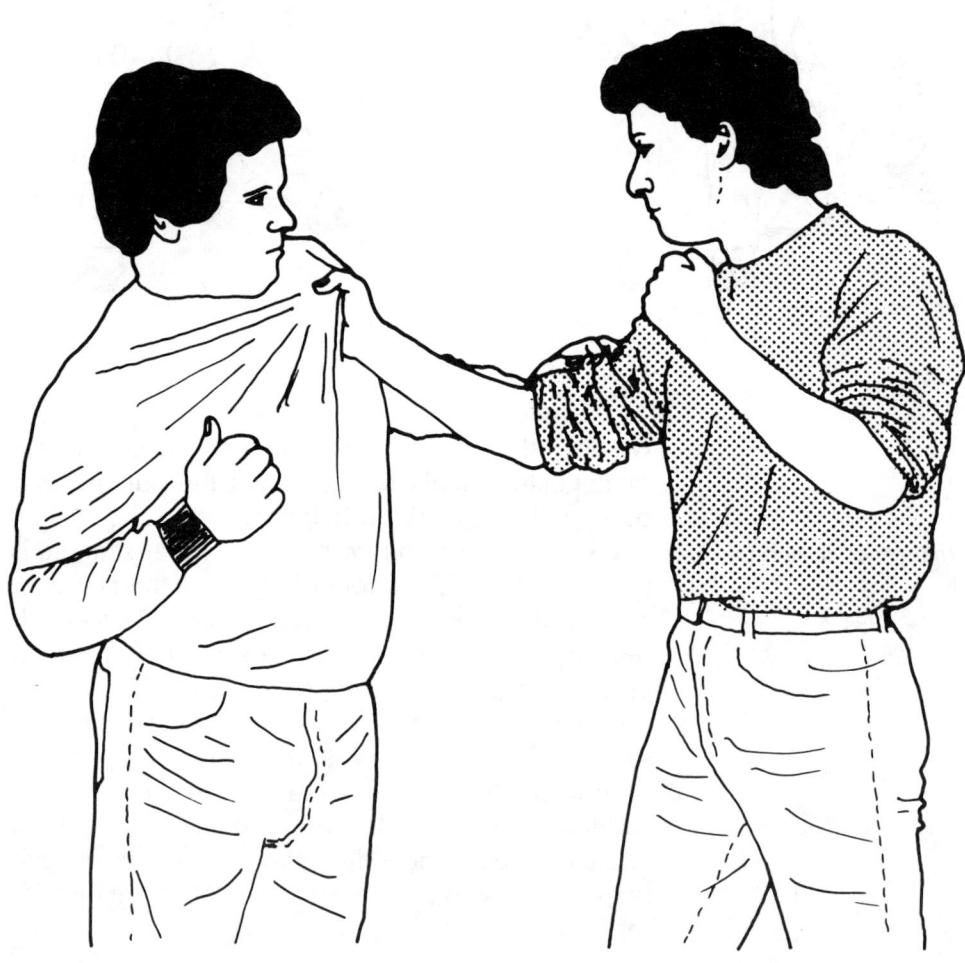

ESCAPES

Double lapel grasps are easier to deal with because tori can use only a head butt or a knee to the groin. The hold is very strong, however, and a lighter uke can be picked up and slammed back into a wall before head butt is used. For this reason, the response must be immediate, with uke reaching up between the pinioning arms to attack tori's eyes with a claw hand. Uke can either continue with the sequence and apply wrist trap, or withdraw to a distance and reapply the principles of distance/evasion and so on.

Claw hand distracts

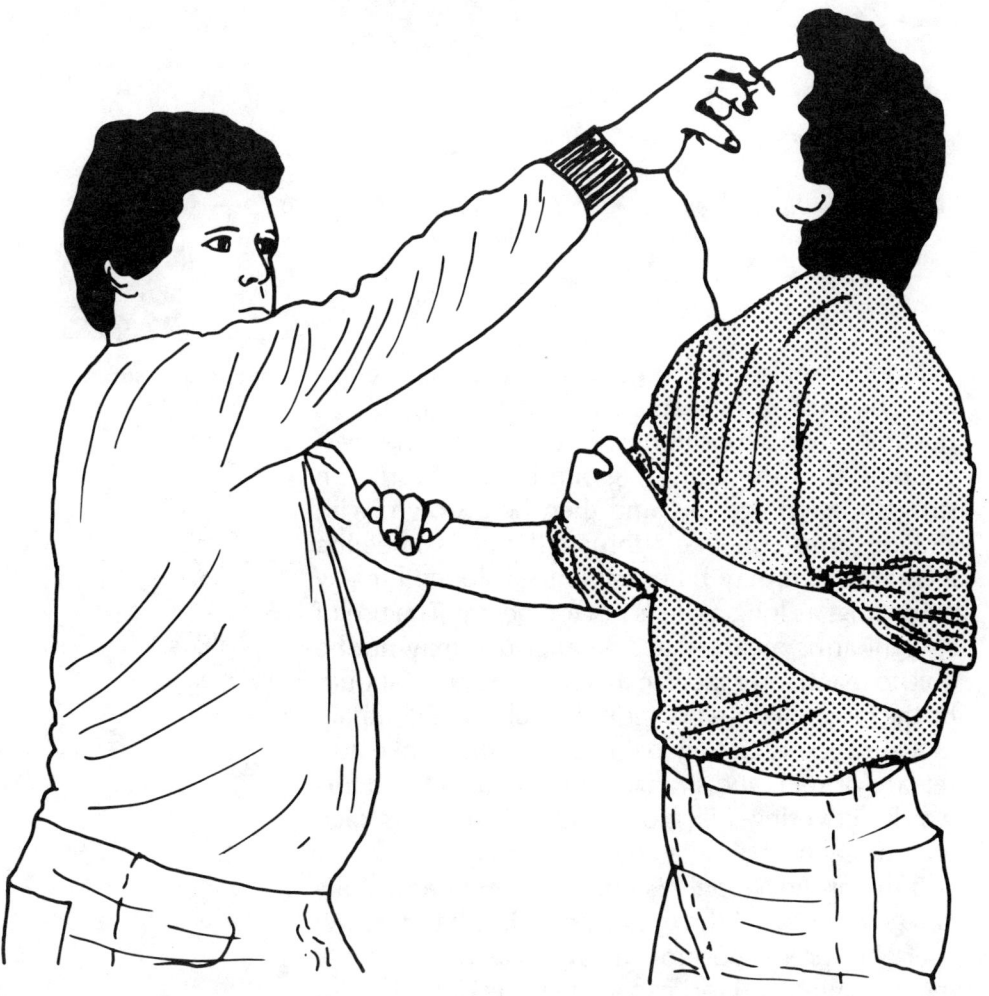

ESCAPES

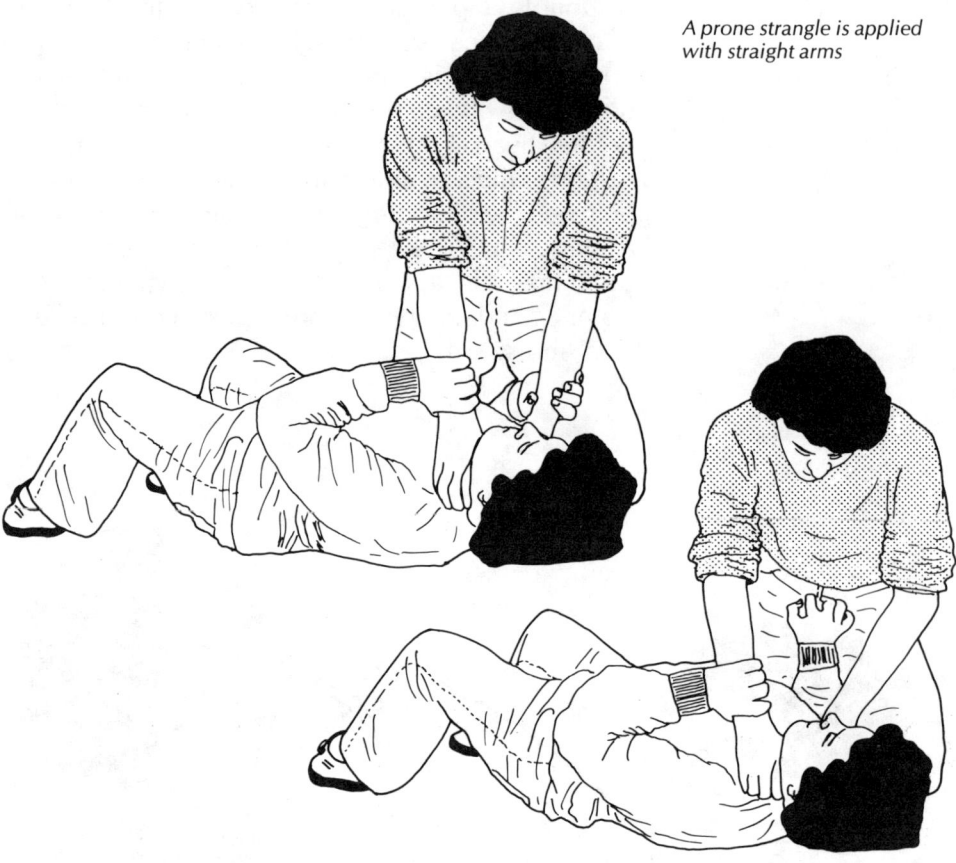

A prone strangle is applied with straight arms

The defender responds by seizing the testicles

Front strangles are dangerous attacks. Every effort must be made to escape from them as quickly as possible. Tori's position will determine the best counter to use. During ground work, tori can struggle on top of uke and then bear down, with straight arms, on uke's throat. If tori is kneeling astride uke, it may be possible to dislodge him by struggling, as long as he is not too heavy. The use of straight arms means that a smaller uke may not be able to reach tori's face. In this case, the groin should be the target. It does not require a substantial impact to cause excruciating pain which will make tori release or relax the strangle. He will also bend forwards, covering his groin and bringing his face within reach of an eye attack.

If the prone strangle is done with bent arms, uke can go directly for the eyes with a claw hand. However, his prone position means that he can only move slowly, and tori can close his eyes and avoid

ESCAPES

injury to the cornea. In this case, the claw hand should be kept in close contact with the face, using the fingers to dig in as hard as possible. The strangle is a very dangerous technique which can easily cause death, so the strongest possible counter-attack can be justified.

Standing strangles are dealt with the same way as lapel grasps. In both cases, uke should make no attempt to wrestle with the confining arms, but use a fast but light strike to tori's eyes with claw hand. If this causes him to relax but not release, a second attack in the form of a knee to the groin can be used. This will prove effective only if it quickly follows the eye strike. Stronger ukes may complete the sequence with a wrist trap.

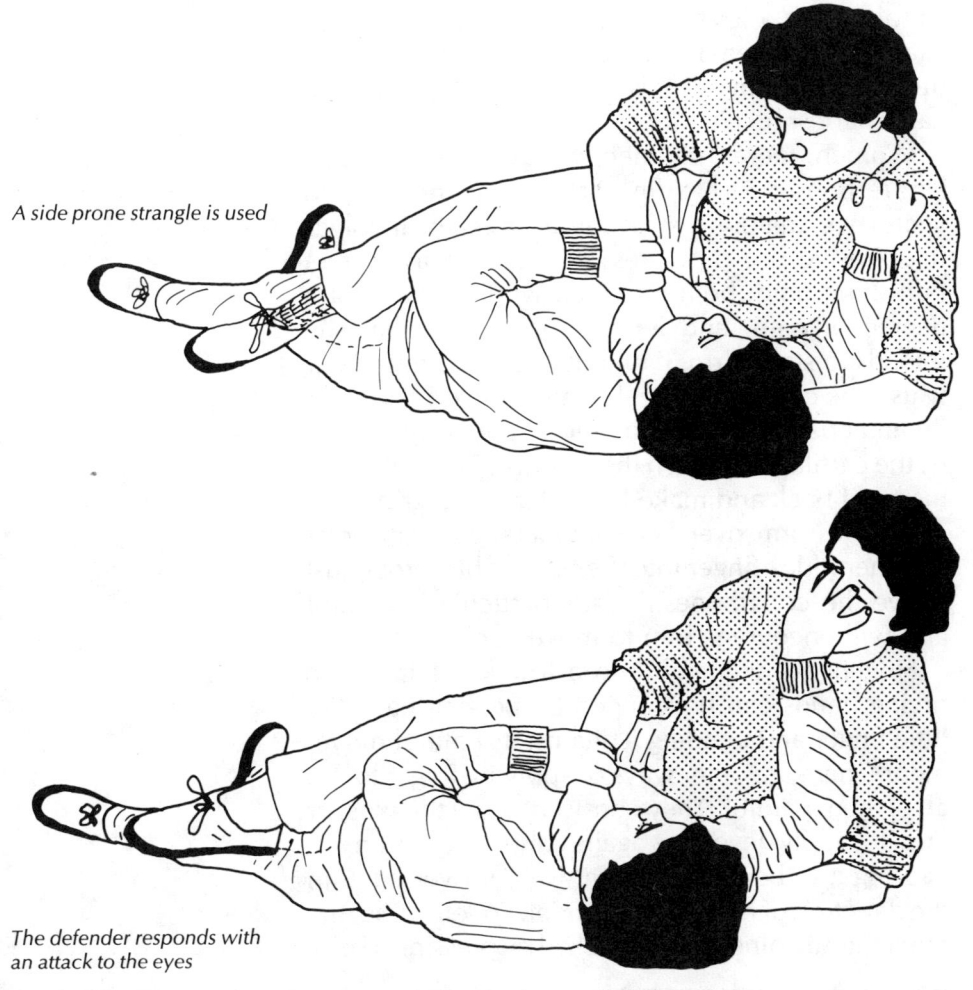

A side prone strangle is used

The defender responds with an attack to the eyes

The sort of thinking needed to work out an escape technique quickly is best learned during ground work, where continuous close range grappling gives many opportunities. Ground work practice should be such that the student can call for a momentary stop at any time, to analyse the particular hold being used. It should not be a meaningless scramble. If the student is unable to work out an escape, the coach should be asked to give advice.

LOW KEY RESPONSES

Not all self defence situations are matters of life or death. It may be that uke decides to put a halt to tori's aggressive behaviour before it flares into actual violence. Alternatively, the surroundings may be such as to require a low key approach — at a party, for example. It is better to try to discourage escalation through reasoning. If this fails, a low key response can establish uke's status.

Women, more than men, will find a use for low key responses in heading off the attentions of an aggressive male. This response typically involves unobtrusive use of a pressure point or a discreet punishing hold, both of which work by causing a degree of pain, and let the man know that she intends to stand firm. If he puts his arm around her waist, she can rest the heel of her hand on his upper lip and push up against the septum of his nose (that is, the cartilage between the nostrils). This will force his head back and make him release the grip. If he drapes his arm over her shoulders, she can press with her index finger into the base of his throat, just above the collarbones. This is particularly painful and will encourage him to move back.

Fingers are vulnerable to a low key attack and prying hands can be stopped by peeling back the little finger and bending it against its natural movement. There are other ways of applying finger locks, all of them painful. They consist of using the wrist or arm to apply leverage against the weaker finger, causing it to bend the wrong way, or over-bend in the direction of normal movement. For example, the outer thumb joint can be attacked by pressing it back against the base. Pressure is applied to the thumb nail by the bight of uke's thumb (the angle where it joins the hand), with the index finger encircling the thumb base. Providing the joint is squeezed so as to force the thumb joint upwards and backwards, pain will be inflicted.

Alternatively, the index finger can hook around the back of a finger, forming a fulcrum against which leverage can be applied to force it back against the joint. With a little practice, it is possible to learn how to apply these painful locks while disguising the initial movements.

In conclusion:
   To escape, attack the eyes or groin first.
   Practise escapes as part of groundwork.
   Low key responses use pressure points and finger locks.

BASIC GROUND WORK

During an attack, both parties may end up scrabbling on the floor, as people involved in fights often lose balance, trip, or are thrown. It is therefore important that any self defence course includes a section dealing with ground work.

When the victim is on the ground, his aim is to

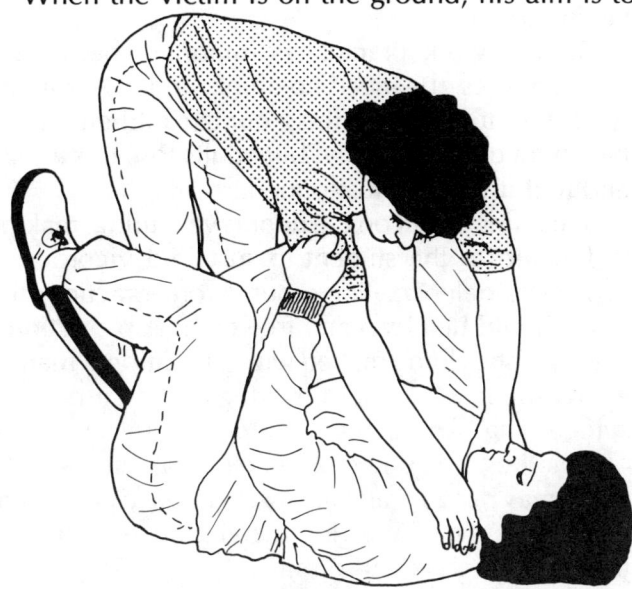

Prone defence position

BASIC GROUND WORK

escape and, if possible, subdue the attacker. Ground work is strictly close range, presenting no possibilities to use special stances from which to launch high energy strikes. It may be possible to use a low energy, short range kick or punch to a vulnerable target, but otherwise only grapples may be employed.

The weaker person on the ground is in a very bad position. It is impossible to maintain a favourable distance and the possibility of evasion is minimal. Strength is pitted against strength and ability against ability. The attacker will try to intimidate a female victim and, once submission is gained, he may go on to sexual assault. The male victim is likely to be injured to such an extent that he cannot prevent the attacker from regaining his feet.

Once on the ground, the attacker may go for a strangulation hold or a head chancery. Neither requires great technical skill but both can be very effective. The strangle, which cuts off blood supply to the brain, can cause unconsciousness or even death. The head chancery is a restraint hold which allows the attacker to gouge the victim's eyes and face. The attacker can also grab at and twist loose arms but, unless he is skilled, this may destabilise him and allow the victim to escape. The attacker will always try to roll on top, using body weight to pin the victim down.

Ground work practice is important because it re-establishes the need to think and co-ordinate while the student is on the ground. Children scramble about quite naturally, but adults lose this ability and find it difficult to respond.

Struggling about on the floor is very tiring, making it difficult for the student to sustain a vigorous, if unskilled, defence. For groundwork practice, the floor should be clean and free of any obstructions. Ideally it should be matted with a traditional martial arts/combat sport floor covering, but a carpet will suffice. The participants should wear loose, casual old clothes, including a jacket. Trainers or light shoes may be worn and it is a good idea to check that neither partner is wearing metal objects or fastenings which might cause injury.

BASIC GROUND WORK

An understanding of some general principles will improve the quality of practice. The first is body positioning. One partner should always try to get on top of the other and, once there, resist attempts to reverse the situation. The legs should be splayed as widely as possible to provide stability and the centre of gravity should be kept as close to the floor as possible. The lighter partner will be more difficult to unseat if he sits on the ground, maintaining a tight hold. It is easier to roll out from underneath if the partner on top is not firmly stabilised. Any loose limbs should be seized and held in a tight grip. A head lock is a good move.

Like the other sections in the MAC training schedule, that on basic groundwork lists six practice techniques. Although these would work only against a weaker, injured, or less agile attacker they form an excellent starting point.

The first practice technique is the pinion. Partner A approaches the prone partner B from the right, looping his right arm over B's left shoulder, under the head. With the fingers of his right hand he takes a firm hold of B's jacket collar. Partner A's left arm traps B's right, grasping it near the elbow. A sits on the mat and leans over B, spreading the legs to give good stability.

Provided a tight grip is maintained, the pinion is very difficult to escape from. Partner B can pull free if he turns in towards A and backs out, but A can prevent this by releasing the neck hold and using the free hand to push against the mat, thus re-stabilising the hold.

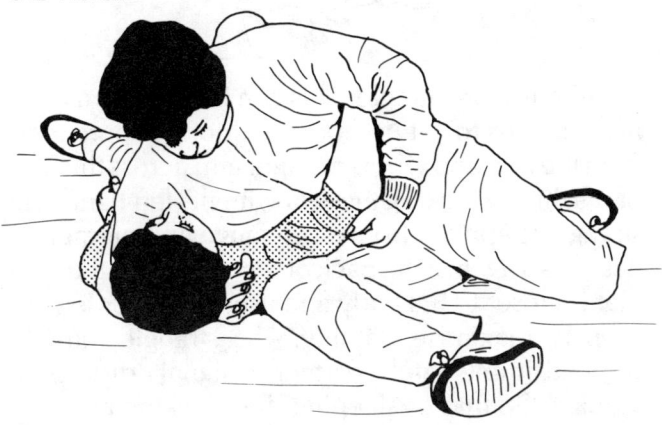

Pinion

BASIC GROUND WORK

The second technique, the hold down, is suitable for the heavier person. In the scramble following a fall to the floor, partner A throws himself over B's head and upper body. A's arms force their way under B's shoulders, extending down until they reach the belt where they take a firm grip. A's knees are as wide apart as possible and his upper body presses down over B's face and chest. Partner B can attempt to escape by reaching around A's arm and grasping the belt, using leverage to twist the body around and out of the hold.

Hold down

Rear strangle

Third is rear strangle. This can be applied as partner B begins to get up from the floor. A approaches from the rear and whips his right arm across the front of B's throat, locking the arm with his left hand. The strangle is applied from close range and partner A's head rests against the back of B's. A rests on the knee that is closer to B's body and uses the other leg as a prop to maximise stability. The strangle must be stopped immediately partner B signals distress by tapping the mat or slapping the blocking arm.

BASIC GROUND WORK

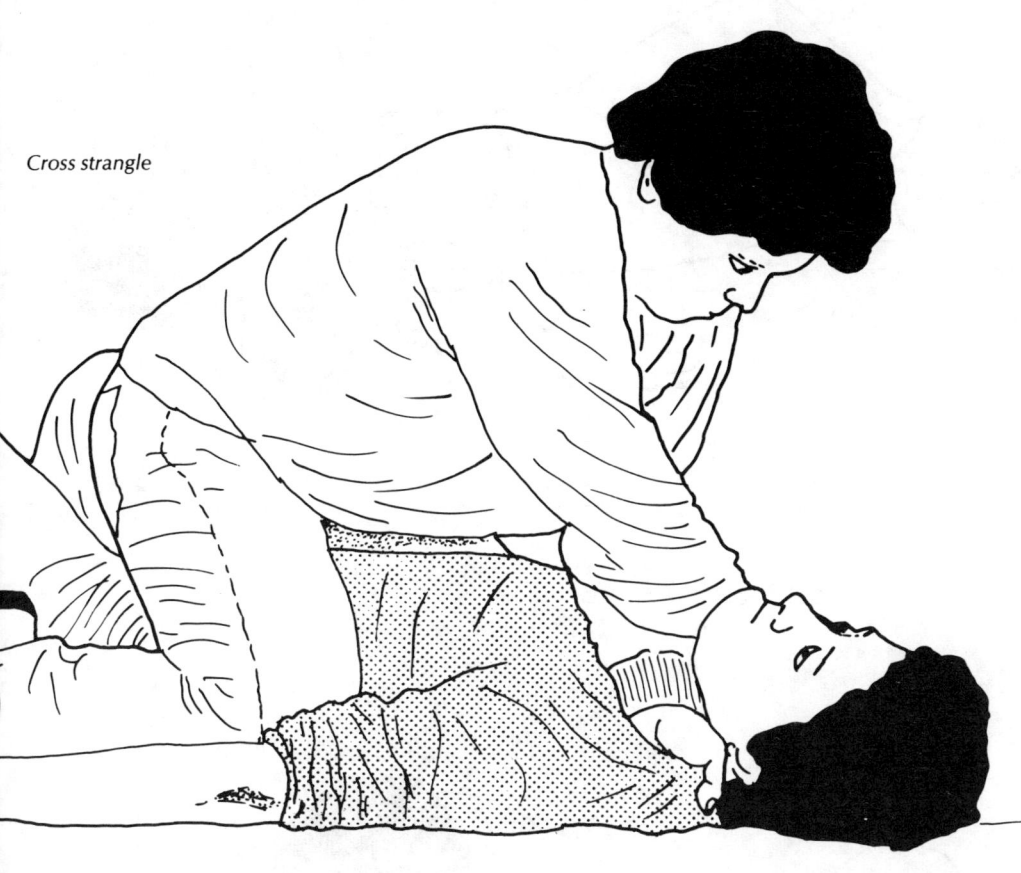

Cross strangle

The fourth technique is cross strangle, which uses partner B's jacket for purchase. Partner A can kneel astride B, or lean across from one side, with the legs widely spread for stability. A grasps first one side of B's jacket collar, then the other, so the neck is caught in a kind of cross block. The lower forearms press against the sides of B's neck and can cut off the blood supply to the brain, bringing about rapid unconsciousness. It is very important to realise that B can pass out without any great fuss; there is danger if his condition is not constantly monitored.

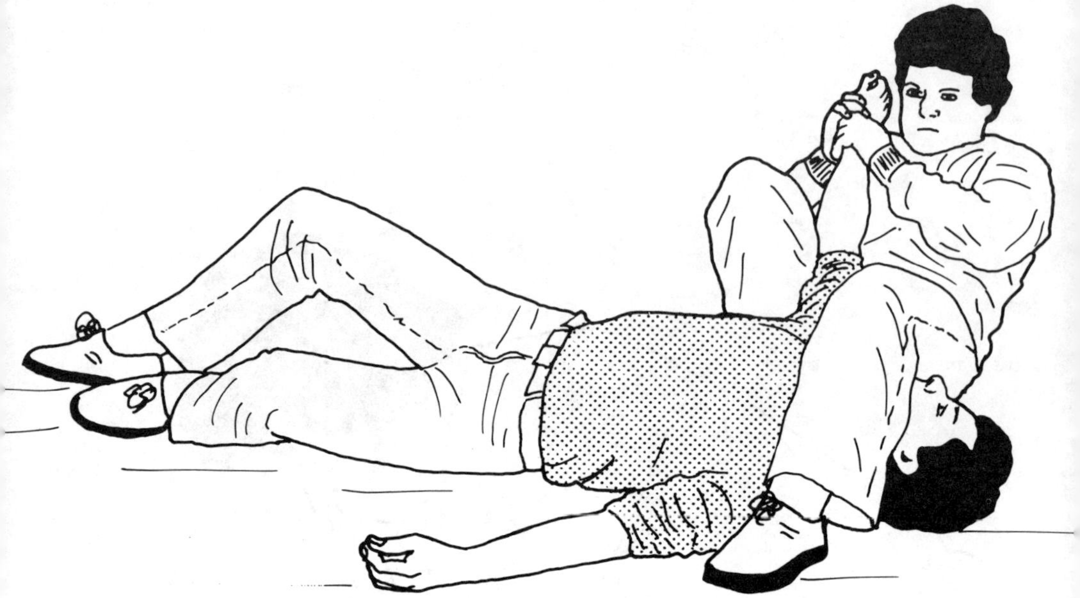

BASIC GROUND WORK

Elbow lock

Armlock

BASIC GROUND WORK

Elbow lock, the fifth technique, can restrain the attacker while the victim keeps his face away from flailing fists and boots. Partner A seizes an outstretched arm by the wrist and leans suddenly back, extending the arm and pulling it back against its natural stop. A's bent left leg comes to lie across B's chin and throat and the right leg acts as a backstop, the shin pressed firmly into B's side. The arm is pulled up and back between A's legs.

To apply armlock, the sixth and last practice technique, partner A approaches B's right side and lies across his chest. A's left hand seizes the wrist of B's bent left arm in an overarm grip, and the other loops under B's upper arm, gripping the attacking left wrist in a second overarm grasp. This applies painful leverage to partner B's elbow.

The partners should practise these six techniques until a reasonable standard of competence is reached. During periods of free practice, an effort should be made to use one or other of them.

The student of self defence should also learn how to fall safely. This is best practised on a mat, to avoid bruises. The judo method of slapping the floor hard on landing is not to be recommended for use on stone or concrete floors. The flailing arm can easily catch something. It is much safer to use a simple version of the aikido roll-out.

The principle of the roll-out is that it transforms vertical motion into horizontal by curving the body and rolling on it. To practise, the student runs and dives forwards into the mat. One arm extends in the direction of fall and contacts the mat first, causing the body to roll over. The head is tucked in below the fending arm and the legs brought up and together. As the student becomes more skilful, the speed and height of the dive can be increased.

If one is violently pushed backwards off balance, it is not a good idea to try to twist round to cushion the landing with outstretched arms. The head should be brought down on to the chest and the fingers interlaced at the back of the neck. The body should curve forwards and one should try to roll backwards on landing. If the stance is correct, the shoulders will take most of the impact. This fall is practised by

BASIC GROUND WORK

simply falling backwards on to the mat, taking care first to check it is safe to do so.

When one is falling to the side, the arm nearer the ground should reach out palm downwards and elbow bent. It must not be straightened, otherwise a Colles fracture can result. The bent arm absorbs the initial landing force and the student attempts to roll away, regaining his feet as quickly as possible.

As a general principle, any fall is made safer if the person can relax, while keeping vulnerable areas out of the way. If a roll-out is impossible, every effort should be made to land on a padded bit of the body.

Once on the floor, the defender should adopt a prone defensive position. He rolls on to his side and faces the attacker. The higher of the knees bends and closes the groin, the elbows guard the midline of the body, and the forearms protect the face. As the attacker moves, so should the defender, constantly

Groundwork pose

swivelling to keep face-on. The fending knee should be used to ward off kicks; though this may prove painful, it is less dangerous than a boot in the head.

It may be possible to keep the attacker at bay by lashing out with the uppermost foot. An experienced martial artist can bring down the attacker by hooking one leg behind his leading ankle and stamping at the knee with the other foot.

There is no defence against a gang of attackers. In this case the only thing the prone defender can do is form a ball, pulling the head right down into the shoulders and folding the arms over the top of it. The feet are brought right up, so the knees are against the chest and one ankle locks behind the other. This partially shields the most vulnerable areas.

SECTION 5 GENERAL ADVICE FOR STUDENTS

PRACTISING SELF DEFENCE

Self defence courses must be carefully evaluated to see whether they are worth joining. They should be checked for realism, and the techniques taught examined for wide application. The instructor must have a nationally recognised qualification which shows he is competent to teach, and would-be students are recommended to practise only at Martial Arts Commission registered clubs. These clubs issue the students with an MAC licence, this being a form of national enrolment embodying a personal accident and third party insurance policy.

If a club is not registered, this need not mean the instructor is incompetent. However, it does mean that the student is taking the instructor's qualifications at face value, and there is no guarantee of redress in the event of unsatisfactory training.

Where no adequate local self defence course exists, the student is recommended to enrol in a martial art/combat sports club. There are more than 4,000 MAC recognised clubs in Britain and numbers are increasing monthly. The student should explain his reasons for joining since this will help the coach tailor training appropriately. While some martial arts contain much that is not immediately relevant to practical self defence, they will all provide a sound basis to which individually practised techniques taken from this book can be added.

Average members of the public are ill equipped to deal with physical confrontations, not being used to facing someone intent on attacking them, so they cannot easily respond. Someone who practises the martial arts/combat sports will be used to sparring with other students and the same degree of mental readjustment is not required if he is the victim of a real attack.

While all the martial arts have a self defence value, some yield a more immediate, if restricted, benefit than others. To assist the student to understand the options, the following pages describe and compare them.

Aikido

Aikido is a Japanese martial art with a strong self defence potential. The word aikido means 'way of all harmony', and this indicates its basically passive nature. It reacts to the attacker's force by accepting and redirecting it to his disadvantage. The cornerstone of its practice rests on the concept of distance – as does self defence.

The aikido student will try to maintain a constant distance just outside the reach of the attacker, who has to over-commit or step forward to make contact. Once the attacker over-commits, the defender evades, then draws out the technique, applying a joint hold to control it. The wrist is the usual target for counter-attack and leverage is applied to force the attacker into submission.

The Tomiki school of aikido uses a sporting competition to develop dexterity in fast, unprogrammed situations. The restrictions of prearranged sparring are avoided because, within certain limits, the attacker is free to act spontaneously and the response is therefore more open. The school also uses a hectic and valuable two-onto-one form of combat which is particularly useful in developing awareness.

Yoshinkan aikido, which specialises in self defence, uses some quite hard techniques in response to an attack. Typically aikido uses locks that work with the joints; Yoshinkan also applies them against the joints. Advanced Yoshinkan classes practise unprogrammed attacks to test the defender's ability. These are unlimited in scope and can include any weapon in the attacker's arsenal.

Traditional aikido is a great deal softer and does not use force to the same extent as either Tomiki or Yoshinkan. It is devoted to the development of technique with a co-operative partner and its full self defence value therefore takes longer to achieve.

None of the schools of aikido use effective strikes and there is little ground work. Distractions analogous to the MAC first echelon strikes are used before grappling techniques are applied. Aikido techniques are fairly complex, relying on precise leverages to obtain an effect. For this reason, there is a long learning period before they can be used without conscious thought.

Aikido is sparsely distributed throughout Britain. Tomiki aikido clubs are in the majority, followed by traditional aikido and Yoshinkan.

Full contact

Full contact is a sporting activity using strikes only. It is a western innovation based on several traditional oriental martial arts. Competitors use boxing gloves and padded boots to deliver full power kicks and punches to the head, face, and body. Matches take place in boxing rings or on matted areas.

Within the limitations imposed by a purely striking system, full contact is an excellent form of self defence, but it requires youth, strength, suppleness, and agility to exploit its full potential. The strong, young person practising full contact quickly becomes extremely competent at self defence. Full contact can both respond to and initiate attacks. An incoming technique will be evaded and countered, and the defender can use a co-ordinated series of strikes similar to the first/second echelon sequences of the MAC course.

Training consists of sparring with partners and using the punch bag to develop speed and power. Despite the title, there is little actual full contact during training; it is only found in competitions.

Full contact is not well distributed throughout Britain.

Hapkido

Hapkido, the Korean equivalent of aikido, also means 'way of all harmony'. It is actually more closely allied to jiu jitsu than aikido, containing as it does the means to initiate attacks as well as respond to them.

Training is in three parts. The first deals with

impact techniques of all types, including spectacular high kicks. These form the attacking part of the syllabus and are identical to those used in other Korean systems. The second part consists of traditional locks and holds of the type found in schools of hard aikido, such as Yoshinkan. This is the responsive part of the syllabus. The third part revolves around the use of distance, compliance, and avoidance, the attacker's force being met and redirected along lines favourable to the defender. There is little ground work.

Though there are competitions, hapkido is mainly concerned with practical self defence. There is a very large syllabus that takes many years to learn in its entirety. Hapkido has a wider application than aikido because of its striking techniques. It is possible to achieve both an early benefit through practice of these techniques and a long-term benefit through knowledge of the locks, holds and throws.

Regrettably, hapkido is not well distributed throughout Britain. It is also known under its umbrella name of sulkido.

Jiu jitsu

Jiu jitsu is a Japanese martial art, the name meaning 'compliant techniques'. Judo, a combat sport developed from it, has shed the more dangerous techniques in the process. Jiu jitsu has one of the largest syllabuses of any martial art and it is still undergoing development. Originally it was used to take swords away from warriors but the modern version is much wider in its application.

Jiu jitsu is concerned solely with self defence, to the virtual exclusion of sport and other aspects. It incorporates such systems as atemi waza, a study of striking techniques applied to vulnerable parts of the body. Whereas a high velocity strike acts like a sledgehammer, the atemi waza strike is lower energy but accurately targeted to a weak point.

Aikido came from jiu jitsu and it is therefore not surprising that they share common techniques. Jiu jitsu is more static, however, and there is less movement in applying locks and holds. There is a large and effective section on ground work and a wide syllabus of throws, including those selected for the MAC course. Low key responses are also practised. For this reason, jiu jitsu is used as the basis for prison officer specialised training, where sometimes violent inmates have to be restrained by means which involve the least likelihood of injury to either party.

The large syllabus means that everyone can take from it those self defence techniques which happen to suit. The training is quite rigorous and requires a fair degree of physical fitness, though special courses are devised for disabled and physically disadvantaged students.

Jiu jitsu is well distributed throughout Britain.

Karate
Karate is an Okinawan martial art which was further developed in Japan to its present form. The name means 'empty hand', a play on words indicating that the only weapons required are those of the human body. Karate has the largest following of all the martial arts practised in Britain. It exists in various styles, each of which emphasises a particular feature of the art. In general terms, karate uses no holds, throws, or ground work; it is a striking system. Its techniques require specialised stances for the delivery of high energy strikes by the hands and feet.

Training is done in class lines or with a partner. Basic techniques are first learned separately and, as ability increases, they are linked together like those of the MAC course. Whole series of combinations are put together into a training form known as the kata. This represents self defence against multiple attackers and it used to be the highest expression of karate practice before the development of karate competition. In sport karate, participants can use any combination of scheduled techniques in an unprogrammed attack pattern. Neither groin kicks nor open hand attacks to the eyes are allowed.

By comparison with the techniques of aikido, for example, those of karate are simple, so the student can reach an elementary level of self defence skill within a very short time.

Shotokan is the most popular style of karate. It is

athletic and powerful, relying upon strong low stances and forceful hand techniques. Wado ryu is lighter and faster, using more upright stances and, curiously, a couple of wrist locks. It stresses distance rather more than other styles, and is more suited to the lighter person. Shukokai is an extremely powerful style which has undergone development comparatively recently. It is committed to the development of strong techniques and uses an impact pad to measure force generated.

Shotokai is a variety of Shotokan, but its movements are performed in an altogether softer manner, more reminiscent of aikido than karate. Its apparent softness is misleading, for it relies on different principles for the development of force. Shotokai students are among the most competent users of distance for tactical advantage. There is no competition, but free sparring is practised by the higher grades.

Sankukai, a small offshoot of Shukokai, is noted for its circular movements. It is still undergoing development and new ways of developing power are being considered. Goju ryu is a traditional style of Okinawan karate with still recognisable links to its kung fu ancestor. Its practice is arduous and involves a traditional form of weight training. Goju students condition the body so the knuckles become calloused like bludgeons. It is probably one of the most effective forms of karate, retaining many of the old and effective grabs and strikes.

Kyokushinkai karate is extremely strenuous and demands a high level of commitment from its students. There is no doubt that it is an effective form of self defence. The practitioners indulge in a particularly demanding competition known as knockdown, where blows of unlimited force are aimed at the body and head.

Karate is well distributed throughout the British Isles.

Kempo

Kempo is the Japanese word for boxing. There are three separate systems, the largest being Shorinji kempo, or 'Shaolin temple boxing'. The Shaolin temple was where the ancient Chinese fighting arts were honed to a pitch of effectiveness. Shorinji kempo is registered as a religion and its followers practise a form of Buddhism called Kongo-zen, or 'mind like a diamond'.

It is a good self defence system, using both striking and grappling techniques. The striking techniques are not particularly powerful but are aimed at vulnerable parts of the attacker's body, just as they are in jiu jitsu. The extremely effective grappling techniques are obviously based on jiu jitsu and aikido moves.

There are infrequent competitions but more frequent free sparring where selected techniques can be practised in an unprogrammed manner. The training aims to build up very fast reactions through lifelike sequences of techniques called embus.

Nippon kempo is a form of Japanese boxing where contestants wear body and head armour for protection against hard blows. Its stress on tactical distancing and body movements to evade techniques is greater than in other martial arts, except aikido and hapkido. Holds and throws are used, but because the contestants wear boxing gloves they are less sophisticated and restricted to trips and crude leverage. Ground work forms part of the syllabus. The unprogrammed sparring is useful from a self defence point of view.

The third form of kempo is a modern invention developed in America and devoted to the concept of self defence. It involves both striking and grappling techniques.

None of the forms of kempo are well distributed throughout Britain.

Kendo
Kendo is the art of Japanese swordfighting. Though it has little first hand application to the unarmed self defence student, its practice does generate aggression, speed, blocking, and distancing – all vital elements to any self defence system. Kendo is not widely distributed throughout Britain.

Kung fu

Kung fu, one of the earliest known systematised forms of martial art, occurs in two forms. The first, which involves strenuous muscular efforts and exertion, is known as 'hard' kung fu; the other, using softer and more flowing techniques, is called 'soft' kung fu. Neither has well developed grappling techniques in comparison with Japanese systems, and there is no ground work.

The hard school is subdivided into northern and southern styles. The northern styles use many kicks and distance as part of their strategy. The white stork school is an example of a northern system and is particularly suitable for the agile and lighter student of self defence. Southern styles, using shorter range and fewer kicks, are useful for the less agile but fairly strong person. Wing chun, a typical style of this school, is highly recommended as a quickly learned and effective basic form of self defence. It employs high powered but short range strikes which are ideal for a close-up confrontation.

The soft school includes tai chi chuan, or 'great ultimate fist'. This is a seemingly relaxed form of boxing practised a great deal by older people. There is little physical evidence of strong movements, yet kung fu masters appear to rate it very highly as a fighting art. Unfortunately, it can take decades to learn how to generate the form of relaxed power necessary to make it work as a self defence system.

Kung fu is fairly well distributed through the south of England and around the larger cities in other parts of the country. Few authentic masters are prepared to teach it to non-Chinese.

Taekwondo

Taekwondo is a Korean martial art developed to its present form in 1955. It is based upon older Korean martial arts used in the country's turbulent past by the warrior caste. Its name means 'hand/foot art' and it is well established as a military form of unarmed combat. It is almost entirely a hard striking system, though one of the schools has a small section which includes some simple locks, holds, and throws.

The art is noted for the variety of its high kicks and for using a form of technique testing in which various thicknesses of wood are broken. The training format is similar to that of karate, with basic techniques, combination techniques, and patterns. There is also a vigorous form of competition. The art probably functions best at a reasonable distance, where the kicks can be used to advantage.

Taekwondo is well distributed throughout Britain.

Tang Soo Do
Tang Soo Do is a Korean martial art similar to Japanese karate. The comments applied to the latter are applicable also to Tang Soo Do, except that it is not so well distributed throughout Britain. Like taekwondo, it is noted for its spectacular kicks.

Thai boxing
Thai boxing is a particularly violent combat sport. It is largely similar to full contact, but differs in that it permits the use of elbows and knees. It is a pure fighting art, and particularly useful as a self defence system. The Thai boxing syllabus contains no grappling techniques and no ground work. It favours young and athletic people, and there is no obligation for them to compete in competitions. The training is similar to full contact.

Thai boxing is not well distributed throughout Britain.

FIT TO PRACTISE

Self defence training involves many repetitions of techniques which are often physically demanding. To cope with this, the student has to develop a suitable level of fitness. This can be achieved through a training programme which will increase suppleness, improve endurance, and sustain maximum exertion.

Suppleness extends the range of joint movement, allowing the student to tolerate more easily the grapples and the demanding techniques. Improved endurance means that the student can cope with the level of physical activity in the self defence class,

FIT TO PRACTISE

being more able to concentrate on the techniques and less on merely trying to last the lesson out. Maximum exertion should be extended for as long as possible, since in an attack, the victim will need to operate at maximum speed and power for as long as it takes to escape or to subdue the attacker.

The most suitable exercises for the course will be demonstrated by the club coach. The complete exercise programme consists of classwork, which is performed before and after the lesson, and homework, where the class exercises are repeated at home. There should be a minimum of three exercise periods a week, each of not less than 20 minutes' duration. If this programme is maintained, the student's level of fitness will gradually rise.

Exercises should not be undertaken after a heavy meal, or after drinking alcohol. People who have not exercised for years should start cautiously and not try to keep up with other, perhaps younger, students. The aim is not to compare performance with others but to work within one's own capabilities; comparison should be limited to the steady improvement in the student's own fitness level. Older students should visit their doctor for a check-up before joining a self defence or martial art class, and should tell the club instructor of any pre-existing health problems.

The classwork exercise programme consists of the warm-up and the cool-down. The purpose of the warm-up is to bring the body's tissues to a state where exertion can be made without damage. Torn muscles and sprains result when the warm-up has been omitted or cut short. It takes oxygenated blood into the limbs where it feeds the muscles during the initial exertions of training. Once they are thoroughly warmed up, heavy training can begin.

The cool-down returns the body from a higher level of physical exertion to normal. It is seen typically in runners who, at the end of a race, put in an extra lap or so at a gradually slowing pace. During muscle operation over long periods, a waste product called lactic acid builds up. In time this is broken down, but while it remains it can cause soreness and stiffness in untrained muscles. The cool-down gives the muscle the opportunity to break down lactic acid at a faster rate by providing light work in a well oxygenated environment. A hot bath following training is another good way to avoid aches and pains.

Both warm-up and cool-down provide exercises to promote suppleness and improve stamina. Suppleness exercises allow the maximum movement of joints within the limits imposed by their structure. This limitation is set at birth and suppleness is gradually lost from puberty onwards. Provided the joints are exercised, deterioration will be slowed. Deterioration occurs through the shortening of tendons with age and the gradual loss of 'give' in the joint capsule and muscle. Suppleness exercises take each joint through its full range of movement in a manner which avoids undue stresses and strains. This is done by relaxed stretching, using the student's own body weight, or by assisted stretching, where a partner applies gradual force to a joint.

Whichever method is chosen, the student must try to relax and feel in control of the situation. Deep breathing is useful, and there should be pauses when the pain barrier is reached. At this point, the muscles of the exercising limb should tense while the position is held. After a count of 10 they can be relaxed, and force applied once more to the joint. After contraction, the muscle seems looser and able to stretch further.

When the furthest limit of joint movement is reached, it should be held for a count of 10 and then eased back. Under no circumstances should the student try to bounce against the joint or to jerk it suddenly; neither will lead to increased suppleness, but both may cause injury.

Stamina training is a programme for increasing the ability of the heart and lungs to cope with physical demands. Typically, this involves periods of low demand physical work such as jogging, leisurely swimming, or cycling. The heart, like any other muscle, becomes flabby if it is not exercised. It becomes inefficient at pumping blood, so the muscles run out of oxygen and begin cramping up at an early stage. The lungs use only a small proportion of their capacity when the body is resting; the chest does not inflate fully and there is a great deal of residual air left after each breath. If the lungs are not regularly encouraged to fill and exhaust to capacity, their tissues can become inelastic and peak ventilation can fall. It is therefore important to ensure that both heart and lungs are exercised regularly.

Maximum output endurance is a way of training the muscles to tolerate the lactic acid which builds up in them during periods of intense physical activity. In an attack, it may be necessary to sustain a maximum effort over a prolonged period of time in order to counter the attacker. This will require maximum output endurance training. Typically this consists of short bursts of high intensity exercise concentrating on specific muscle groups. After the briefest of pauses, exercise follows exercise in a pattern known as circuit training.

Every exercise programme begins with the warm-up. At the start of the class, the coach will have students running on the spot and raising their knees high, or jumping and tucking the knees against the chest. After a minute or two of this exercise, the class will switch to press-ups. The students support their bodies clear of the floor on straight arms and tiptoes. Each body must be in a straight line from heels to back of head, with no sagging in the middle or pushing the bottom up. On command, the students lower themselves by bending their elbows until their chests graze the floor. During this time, the face must be turned slightly forward. Once the body is at its lowest point, the arms push it back to the start position, ready to repeat the press-up at the next count.

Women may find that their chest and arm muscles are insufficiently developed to do press-ups in this manner. In that case, they should assume the same starting position and then lower their knees to the floor. Keeping the back straight, they should then proceed as for a full press-up. Both men and women should aim to do at least 20 press-ups.

The next exercise is the sit-up. It is important to perform this with the knees bent, otherwise injury can be caused to the lower back. The students lie on their backs, with feet tucked under a wall bar or held down by partners. The arms are folded behind the head and the shoulders lie flat on the floor. At the command, the students raise their shoulders clear of the ground. The elbows move forwards and touch the knees at the top of the sit-up. The body is then lowered until it is flat again, awaiting the next call. Students should aim at doing 20 sit-ups.

Burpees are excellent for warming the body up quickly. The students stand upright with feet slightly apart and arms hanging loosely at the sides. On command, they drop into a full crouch with the hands flat on the floor and heels clear. Without hesitation, the feet are driven out backwards to their fullest extent and then quickly brought back in again. From crouch, the students jump straight up into the air with both feet clearing the ground. On landing, they resume the start position and wait for the next command to repeat the cycle. Students must aim at being able to perform 20 burpees.

After this, the body should be warm enough to begin stretching exercises. The student should stand with feet wide apart and lower the body over one leg. The weight-bearing leg bends into a full squat and the body leans forward to prevent loss of balance. The other leg is fully extended and rests on the heel, with the toes pointing up into the air. There should be no bouncing on the bent leg; body weight alone will suffice to stretch the muscles. This exercise is repeated five times on each leg.

The student then sits down and opens the legs as wide as possible, keeping the backs of the knees flat on the floor. At no time during the exercise should they be raised. The student then leans forward and stretches the arms out in front, palms down towards the floor. The object is to reach forward as far as possible. The head must be pulled back and kept looking directly forward. The arms must be kept clear of the floor and breathing should be regular, with muscles relaxed as much as possible. The lowest position reached should be held for a count of 10 and the more supple members of the class can sweep the extended arms from side to side instead of simply pushing forwards. The exercise should be repeated five times.

There is an interesting variation of this exercise which can be practised at home. The student lies on his back parallel to a clear wall and lifts both legs together. Turning the body until the bottom is pressed against the skirting board, the legs are allowed to open out under the influence of gravity. The knees are kept absolutely straight and the hips aligned so the full weight of the legs bears down on the hip joints. Every effort should be made to relax during the exercise and quite surprising increases in hip suppleness will be seen after a short time.

The students then stand up and straighten the legs, keeping the feet a short distance apart. They lean over and down, with the arms reaching down to the floor, upper body weight supplying the force necessary to droop ever lower. Breathing should be calm and controlled and the muscles at the back of the legs relaxed. Once the lowest position has been reached, the leg muscles should be contracted, though without change of body position. After a short period, they are again relaxed; it will now be found that the body can lower a bit more.

In the next exercise, the left leg is put forward and the hands rested on the hips. With the weight on the back leg, the upper body is arched backwards and the head thrown back. This position is held for a count of 10 and then performed again with the other leg forward. The exercise is performed five times on each side.

With the feet wider apart, the elbows are bent and the forearms carried parallel with the floor. The upper body is then twisted, first to one side, then the other, craning the neck to look as far behind as possible. Finally, the whole trunk is rotated in a large circle, with the hands joined above the head. Starting from a bent forwards position with the fingertips brushing the floor, the body swings to one side, carries on up and back as far as possible until it has completely circled around to the start position. The next trunk circle goes in the opposite direction. The exercise is repeated five times in each direction.

In the next exercise the arms are windmilled, moving both in the same direction, forwards and backwards, and then in opposite directions. Following this, they are held palm down just below the chin and flung backwards and out, rotating palm up as they reach the extremity of travel. To maintain balance, one leg should be placed in front of the other.

The final exercise involves the neck joints. The head is allowed to loll forwards on the chest and then lifted up and craned back, only to fall forwards again. After five repetitions, the head is rotated so the face turns first to one side, then to the other. Finally, the head rolls in a circle, first one way, then the other.

At the conclusion of these exercises, the student is fully warmed up and able to begin self defence training. The cool-down at the end of the evening's training repeats the press-ups, sit-ups, burpees, and running on the spot.

Between lessons, the student should continue exercising. He is recommended to run a measured distance of one and a half miles, at least three times a week, aiming for a completion time of less than 13 minutes. This, with the class exercises, will develop a fitness level suitable for the self defence course.

SAFE TO PRACTISE

The practice of any martial art, combat sport, or self defence course includes a risk of injury. This arises from the nature of the techniques taught and the limitations of the students using them. Students should be well aware of this before they enrol, but the level of risk can be reduced by observing simple rules of safety.

In the first instance, students should be physically capable of doing the course. The level of fitness required may exceed the student's capabilities, so students should ensure that they are fit before enrolling. Those over 40 are urged to have a full medical before starting the course.

Some medical disabilities affect the student's safety in the training hall, but only one rules training out altogether. Anyone who suffers from haemophilia and related diseases should not try to enrol on any self defence course. Epileptics can train provided the floor of the practice hall is padded. Cardiac sufferers will find training beneficial as long as they operate within their own limits and stop immediately at the onset of angina. Diabetics should make allowances for heavy exercise and ensure they have sugar available. Asthmatics will find training very beneficial; there are recorded instances of this condition improving greatly as a result of regular training.

The club coach must be informed of any health problem so he can make the appropriate allowances. Students who join MAC recognised self defence courses will receive a Martial Art Commission licence. This incorporates a personal accident policy which can be invalidated if a student fails to declare a health problem.

Young students can be taught self defence of a specialised type. They will not be taught eye strikes or groin kicks, but will be shown how to escape from holds applied by people of their own age and size. They will also be taught throwing and ground work. The coach will give special attention to them and there may well be special classes arranged. 'Problem' youngsters can also be taught self defence but its format will be altered from the course contained in this book. There is some evidence to suggest that practising a discipline of a martial art type can have beneficial results in these cases.

As soon as students join an approved club, they will be given an application form for a Martial Arts Commission licence. This must be completed immediately and returned to the club coach for him to send to the MAC. Provided the coach observes the normal rules concerning MAC licence issue, students are covered by insurance as soon as they hand completed forms and the required sum of money to the coach.

Insurance protects not only the licence-holder, but the other students too. Despite the best supervision in the world, accidents happen. Insurance provides consolation if not protection at these times.

When training, the student should make sure that he is well away from obstacles such as chairs, pillars, radiators, and shelves. Low light fittings, windows, and glass doors near the training area should also be avoided. Training must be on mats, since throws can bring someone down to the ground with a substantial bump.

The mat should not be overcrowded, especially during throwing practice. Serious injury can result if people train in crowded conditions. When someone is about to be thrown, tori should check the mat first to see that there is a clear landing space. Uke should not be thrown off the edge of the mat, nor into an obstacle. All students should be practising the same technique so there is no chance of anyone being landed on while he is practising ground work.

Before training, there should be a proper warm-up. The student should not have eaten a heavy meal or drunk alcohol immediately beforehand. Clothes should be loose and comfortable and have no metal fastenings or suchlike which might cause injury to the partner. Jewellery should be removed before training. A signet ring can produce a nasty laceration, so those which cannot be removed should be taped over. A snagged neck chain can cut the neck deeply. Ear-rings can be torn out of ears during ground work, so it is wise to remove them before coming on to the mat. Contact lenses, spectacles, and watches should be removed lest they be lost or damaged.

Care should be taken when practising with people who are much larger or heavier. Even a light technique can be powerful when it is applied by a large person, and a badly controlled technique can cause injury. This is not to say that practice should be restricted to partners of one's own weight and size, but merely that care should be taken and allowances made when doing otherwise.

Students are expected to enjoy training, and a light-hearted approach does not detract from speedy learning — but this does not mean larking about. Some techniques can cause injury if they are not controlled properly, and students should resist the temptation to experiment with them. The coach will always be pleased to offer comments or advice.

Protective clothing can be worn if desired. Men

may find a cricketer's box useful, and women may wear a sports bra. Fist protectors allow the hands to be opened, but cover the knuckles with a layer of absorbent foam. They are useful when using the impact pad, as they prevent abrasion of the skin. Shin and instep pads, which can be worn during kicking practice, can be pull-on elasticated tubes with padding on the front, or open lengths of padding secured by Velcro straps.

THE MARTIAL ARTS COMMISSION

Oriental martial arts and combat sports have been in Britain for many years. Jiu jitsu was established here in the 1920s and judo in the 1950s. Karate became nationally organised in the mid '60s and kung fu, during the early '70s. Judo is an Olympic sport, and taekwondo has recently been accepted as a recognised sport by the International Olympic Committee.

During the '70s, Bruce Lee came to the screen in a series of films that catapulted the martial arts into the limelight. There were two kung fu records in the hit parade and it seemed everyone was practising. Membership swelled to more than a hundred thousand, far more than the existing clubs could cope with. As a result, many clubs were set up by people having little or no true knowledge of the martial arts.

It soon became clear that dangerous techniques could be taught by incompetent instructors. A so-called karate murder awakened the Government to problems associated with uncontrolled martial art practice, and so the Martial Arts Commission was set up, following discussions between the Home Office, Department of Environment, Sports Council, and representatives of the martial arts. The Commission was to produce an overall national licensing system which would identify competent instructors and register individual students. By this means, about 80 separate schools of martial art would be united in one organisation in the same way that the

British Standards Institution kitemark provides a single symbol of quality for a range of different products.

The Martial Arts Commission is a voluntary body. Its members belong to it because they choose to. They are prepared to adopt high standards of practice and will hold themselves liable for complaints. The Commission has no authority of itself, but relies on the good sense and support of the public, local authorities, and media.

Not all martial arts practised in Britain belong to the Commission. A few do not choose to be associated; others are not of a standard to warrant membership. These organisations carry on their own activities to their own standards, and any certificate of competence conferred is valid only within that particular organisation. Unless legislation is introduced, this situation will remain.

The Commission will be pleased to answer any queries on the martial arts, combat sports, and self defence. Enquirers should write (enclosing a stamped, self-addressed envelope) to The Martial Arts Commission, 1st Floor, Broadway House, 15/16 Deptford Broadway, London, SE8 4PE.

ABOUT THE BOOK

The official Martial Arts Commission self defence course is the product of more than 150 years of experience in different martial arts. Unlike most books, it does not present a self defence system from the viewpoint of a single martial art; its raw material has been garnered from aikido, jiu jitsu, karate, and kung fu. Each has contributed special techniques and approaches which make the book unique.

The Martial Arts Commission is grateful to the panel of senior martial artists who gave so willingly of their time and expertise to produce the MAC course.

Brian Eustace
Brian Eustace is a 6th dan in tomiki aikido and holds a black belt in judo. He is the chief instructor of the British Aikido Association, the largest association in membership of the governing body and a founder member of the Martial Arts Commission. He is a Home Office appointed instructor responsible for training police self defence instructors. He has originated a special police self defence system known as taiho jutsu, based upon a mixture of aikido and judo. This has been accepted as the standard form of police self defence in all but the

ABOUT THE BOOK

London Metropolitan force. Mr Eustace was responsible for organising the various contributions into a structured training course.

Edwin Stratton
Edwin Stratton is a 6th dan in shudokan aikido, this being a development from the Yoshinkan school. He is also a judo black belt and trained for a while with the Tokyo riot police in Japan. He is internationally recognised as an expert in self defence and is a consultant lecturer to the United States Karate Association's police training scheme.

Tommy Morris
Tommy Morris, a 6th dan in shukokai karate, is the principal of an international self defence company, Countermeasures Inc. He lectures nationally and internationally on self defence and has set up numerous training programmes for clients. He is an expert with modern weaponry.

Ronnie Colwell
Ronnie Colwell is a 6th dan in shotokan karate. He is an expert in security work and is an accomplished unarmed combat instructor. He has a wide knowledge of jiu jitsu and traditional weaponry.

Dick Morris
Dick Morris, an 8th dan in jiu jitsu, is chairman of the British Jiu Jitsu Association, a founder member of the Martial Arts Commission. He also holds a black belt in judo and is an expert with the baton and traditional weaponry. Like Edwin Stratton, he is a consultant lecturer to the US Karate Association's police training scheme, and is also a co-founder of the World Jiu Jitsu Federation.

Simon Lau
Simon Lau is one of Britain's leading exponents of wing chun kung fu. He has developed this already effective system into a brilliant fighting art and is known for his knowledge of short range high-energy strikes.

David Mitchell
David Mitchell is general secretary of the Martial Arts Commission. He holds a 3rd dan in karate and has also trained in judo and kung fu. He was responsible for writing the book, adding his own ideas, and editing those of the distinguished panel of contributors.

USEFUL CONTACTS

AIKIDO
Mr B Eustace
368 Birmingham Road
Stratford-upon-Avon
Warks
(Self defence and aikido)

Mr E Stratton
Wheelfarm House
Berry Down
Combe Martin
North Devon
(Self defence and aikido)

Mrs S Timms
6 Halkingcroft
Langley
Slough
Berks
(Aikido)

FULL CONTACT
Mr M Haig
145 Birchfield Road
Aston
Birmingham 19
(Full contact)

Mr J Holmes
49 Lapworth Court
Blomfield Villas
London W2
(Full contact)

HAPKIDO
Mr M Kim
NSA Gymnasium
472 Caledonian Road
London N7
(Sulkido and traditional Korean studies)

JIU JITSU
Mr R Clark
British Jiu Jitsu Association
Barlows Lane
Fazakerley
Liverpool 12
(Jiu jitsu and self defence)

Mr R Morris
London Jiu Jitsu Centre
73c Stoke Newington Church Street
London N6
(Jiu jitsu and self defence)

KARATE
English Karate Council
1st Floor, Broadway House
15/16 Deptford Broadway
London, SE8 4PE
(Karate and self defence in England)

Mr O Brunton
89 Brooke Drive
Belfast 11
(Karate and self defence in Northern Ireland)

Mr R Colwell
2 Ribble Road
Gateacre
Liverpool 25
(Karate and self defence in England)

Mr K Mumberson
Smalldrink
Parsonage Lane
Begelly
Kilgetty, Dyfed
(Karate and self defence in Wales)

USEFUL CONTACTS

Mr D Bryceland
74 Lamington Road
Glasgow, G52 2SE
(Karate and self defence in Scotland)

Mr T Morris
Omega Sportplex
68 Glassford Street
Glasgow, G1 1UP
(Karate and self defence in Scotland)

KUNG FU
The Hon. Secretary
British Kung Fu Council
Mr R Eagle
Oakdale Ave
Pinner Road
Northwood
Middlesex HA6 1PG
(Kung fu and self defence)

SHORINJI KEMPO
Mr R Jarman
31 Fairlawn Grove
Chiswick
London W4
(Shorinji kempo)

TAEKWONDO
Mr T McCallum
Rhee's Taekwondo Academy
230 Renfrew Street
Glasgow 3
(Taekwondo and self defence)

Mr J Ingram
53 Geary Road
Gladstone Park
London NW10
(Taekwondo and self defence)

TANG SOO DO
Mr M Loke
22 Parkway Close
Eastwood
Leigh-on-Sea
Essex
(Tang soo do)

THAI BOXING
Mr J Barker
63 Carr Meadow
Willow Vale
Clayton Brook
Preston, PR5 8HR
(Thai boxing)

Mr M Zamities
1 Tideswell Close
Staveley
Chesterfield
Derbyshire
(Thai boxing)

THE MAC SELF DEFENCE COURSE COMPLETE SYLLABUS

1 *Theory*
Lecture on self defence including
   The law
   Weapons
   Realism
   Assertion
   Awareness and avoidance
   Safety

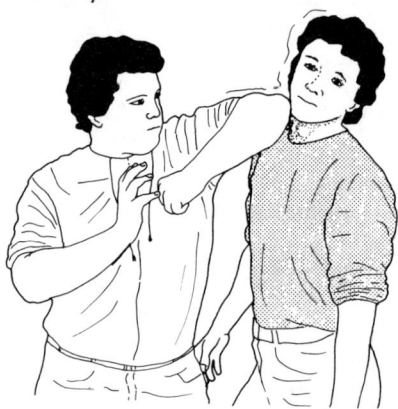

The elbow strike (see page 54)

The groin kick (see page 55)

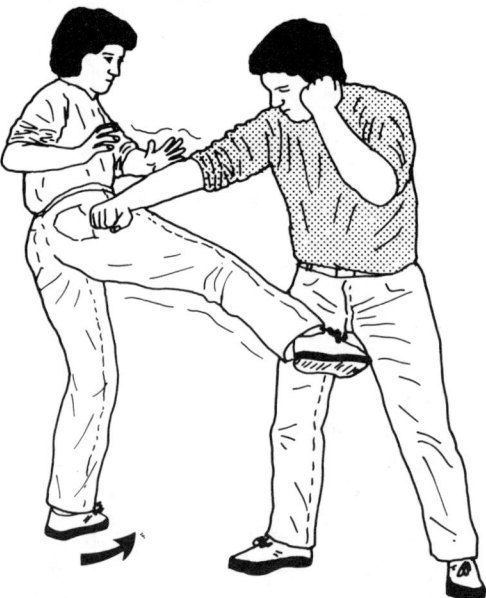

2 *Practical (1)*
  a Warm-up exercises

  b Stance
     Aware stance
     Ready stance
     Cat stance

  c Timing, evasion and blocking

  d Basic weapons and development of force

     Reverse punch
     Snap punch
     Short range punch
     Hammerfist
     Claw hand
     Palm heel
     Finger flick
     Elbow
     Knee
     Snap kick
     Thrusting kick
     Turning kick
     Head butt

  e Targets
     Eyes
     Nose
     Side of jaw
     Throat
     Chest
     Solar plexus
     Groin
     Knees
     Instep

  f First echelon responses
     Fend off/eye strike
     Fend off/claw hand
     Fend off/snap kick
     Cross block/eye strike
     Cross block/claw hand
     Cross block/snap kick

THE MAC SELF DEFENCE COURSE COMPLETE SYLLABUS

3 *Practical (2)*
   a Basic second echelon techniques

   A STRIKING
   Fend off/elbow
   Fend off/palm heel or reverse punch
   Fend off/turning kick
   Cross block/elbow
   Cross block/palm heel or reverse punch
   Cross block/thrust or snap kick

   B GRAPPLING
   Fend off/wrist trap
   Fend off/wrist twist
   Fend off/push down
   Cross block/backwards trip
   Shoulder throw
   Wrist circle

   b Practical responses
   Fend off/eye strike/turning kick
   Fend off/claw hand/wrist twist
   Fend off/turning kick/wrist trap
   Cross block/eye strike/turning kick
   Cross block/claw hand/backwards trip
   Cross block/snap kick/push down

   c Escapes
   Side headlock escape
   Rear strangle escape
   Single lapel grasp escape
   Double lapel grasp escape
   Front strangle escape
   Prone strangle escape

   d Low key responses

   e Basic ground work
   Pinion
   Hold down
   Rear strangle
   Cross strangle
   Elbow lock
   Arm lock

   f Practical ground work
   Prone defence position
   Free practice

   g Cool-down exercises

Backwards trip (see page 107)

Prone strangle escape (see page 116)

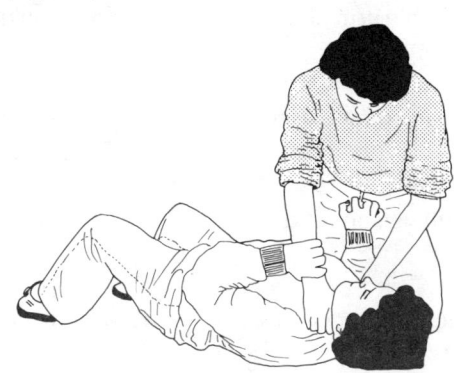

151

SIMPLE ANALYSIS OF ATTACKS AND RESPONSES

Situation	Comments	Response
Attacker closes	–	Maintain distance or evade
Attacker swings punch	–	Evade and use dead time
Attacker straight punches	Part of flurry	Make safe and await opening
Single hand grab to lapel	Punch probably follows	Immediate first echelon strike
Double hand grab to lapel	Butt or knee follows	Immediate first echelon strike
Wrist or arm is grabbed	Victim dragged away	First echelon strike plus wrist twist
Victim is lifted and carried	No further attack possible at that time	Struggle hard and await being set down before countering
Wrist or arm is twisted	Fracture/dislocation possible	Submit and await opening
Single arm choke used	Punch may follow	Immediate first echelon strike
Double arm choke used	Suffocation ensues	Immediate first echelon strike
Rear strangle used	Suffocation ensues	Immediate claw hand to groin
Full nelson used	Restraint hold	No effective counter: await opening
Head chancery used	Restraint/attack hold	Claw hand to groin and break free